Books by Patrick MacGill and published by Caliban Books:

CHILDREN OF THE DEAD END
THE RAT PIT
MOLESKIN JOE
LANTY HANLON
GLENMORNAN
THE GREAT PUSH
THE RED HORIZON
THE NAVVY POET

THE
NAVVY POET:

The Collected Poetry
of
Patrick MacGill

CALIBAN BOOKS

© Patrick MacGill
Caliban Books, 25 Nassington Road, London NW3
1984

Hardback ISBN 0 904573 99 0
Paperback ISBN 1 850660 01 8

Library of Congress Cataloging in Publication Data

MacGill, Patrick, 1890- The navvy poet.

I. Title. PR6025.A23A6 1984   823'.912   84-12751
ISBN 0-904573-99-0

Published in the United States
by Caliban Books, 51 Washington Street,
Dover, New Hampshire 03820
Library of Congress Cataloguing in
Publication Data applied for

Printed and bound in Great Britain by Mackays of Chatham

The following volume represents the
complete republication of MacGill's
previously published books of poetry
Songs of Donegal,
Songs Of The Dead End,
and *Soldier Songs*
and is a facsimile of the
original editions
published in 1921, 1912 and 1917.

SONGS OF DONEGAL

DEDICATION

I SPEAK with a proud tongue of the people who
    were
And the people who are,
The worthy of Ardara, the Rosses and Inish-
    keel,
My kindred—
The people of the hills and the dark-haired
    passes
My neighbours on the lift of the brae,
In the lap of the valley.

To them Slainthe !

I speak of the old men,
The wrinkle-rutted,

7

Who dodder about foot-weary—

For their day is as the day that has been and
is no more—

Who warm their feet by the fire,

And recall memories of the times that are gone ;

Who kneel in the lamplight and pray

For the peace that has been theirs—

And who beat one dry-veined hand against
another

Even in the sun—

For the coldness of death is on them.

I speak of the old women

Who danced to yesterday's fiddle

And dance no longer.

They sit in a quiet place and dream

And see visions

Of what is to come,

Of their issue,

Which has blossomed to manhood and woman-
hood—

And seeing thus

They are happy

For the day that was leaves no regrets,

And peace is theirs

And perfection.

I speak of the strong men

Who shoulder their burdens in the hot day,

Who stand in the market-place

And bargain in loud voices,

Showing their stock to the world.

Straight the glance of their eyes—

Broad-shouldered,

Supple.

Under their feet the holms blossom,

The harvest yields.

And their path is of prosperity.

I speak of the women,

Strong-hipped, full-bosomed,

Who drive the cattle to graze at dawn,

Who milk the cows at dusk.

Grace in their homes,

And in the crowded ways

Modest and seemly—

Mothers of children !

I speak of the children

Of the many townlands,

Blossoms of the Bogland,

Flowers of the Valley,

Who know not yesterday, nor to-morrow,

And are happy,

The pride of those who have begot them.

And thus it is,

Ever and always,

In Ardara, the Rosses and Inishkeel—

Here, as elsewhere,

The Weak, the Strong, and the Blossom-
       ing—

And thus my kindred.

To them Slainthe.

CONTENTS

THE RACHARY WOR

SAID Peadar the Rachary Wor, God rest him !
Man alive and no one could best him—
His back wouldn't bend to the heaviest load,
And his feet were as sure on the rise as the
    road,
Foot-certain and fit on the hill and the bog—
(For the level the pup and the rough the old
    dog).

Born and bred in Rossnagull,
Where the kindly man is never dull,
Where the cattle are good and the pastures
    prime,
Where no woman is old before her time.

And Peadar ! No beast of his stock was thin,
No hole in his roof let the water in.
For harvest he prayed 'neath the cloudy sky
But sharpened his scythe ere the storm was by.

And his friend : the neighbour, whose word of
    grace,
Brought a smile of hope to the widow's face,
And whose step was the ready step to the side
Of the friend by misfortune sorely tried—
And if this was his own for his friend, to claim,
He never stood much on his colour or name.

And Peadar at Fair. . . . The mart was full
Of his mountain sheep and mountain wool,
Branded and ribbiged, wether and ewe,
A man of substance whom everyone knew—
With his gnarled fingers against his hips,
His coloured dudheen between his lips.

Woollen wrapper and woollen socks,
Bawnagh-brockhagh.   Keeper of Flocks !
My ! how he stood in the market town,
Paying in guineas money down ;
Ready to bargain and ready to spend
Or stand a drink to a drouthy friend.

A man whom the neighbours spoke about
As they stood at the bar and drank their
        stout,
Wishing the Man of Flocks increase
Who had not his heart in the penny piece.

Strong was his house.   In all things handy
Thatching a haystack or mending a pandy
Cement in a bargain.   His word was bond
In his own townland and many beyond.
In warranty certain.

When he departed

All his neighbours were broken-hearted

And they gathered together and pondered o'er

The Word and Wisdom of Rachary Wor.

For thus he spoke :

'Twas me to discover

That we twist the same rope over and over.

Faith and Charity, Love and Hope

Show in the strand of the meanest rope,

And the Seven threads of Deadly Sin

Are set in the line that all men spin.

For all is the same for us, man and men,

On the lift of the hill, in the lap of the Glen—

We come and we go, but the end is sure.

Kind word, act and purpose.   These three
    endure—

For 'tis digging of graves and sowing of corn
Now as on the day we were born.

What do we know and What have we thought ?
Much, but never as much as we ought.
This thing or that thing ?   Read me the riddle,
And on knotted strings, come play the fiddle !
Life is a journey, but once to make—
Not great for the foes but the friends we make.

Not even here nor in any town
Is the place for the man whose lips hang
    down,
Whose bitter look and jeering tone
Cuts to the heart and bites to the bone—
For three are the things that come from the
    devil :
The tongue, the eye and the mind that is evil.

Cursed be he of blood and name
Who jokes abroad of a woman's shame—
And scant is their welcome at heaven's door
Who envy the worthy and scorn the poor.

Worthy your deed ! But no one knew
In your own townland what was done by you—
Now close your lips on your deed of shame,
But seven townlands will speak your name—
Though the worthy deed may be chained to its
    seat
The deed that is evil has supple feet.

Thus far, now further. Take heed once more
To the Word and Wisdom of Rachary Wor.

Three things accursed. The Gambling Den,
The Whisky Bottle, the Lawyer's Pen.

Once to the hazard ! And Once calls Twice

To win on the Cards what you lost on the Dice.

Winning ! A gift ? No : the luckless bait

That drags you to ruin soon or late—

For this, the say and the word of sense :

Your profit is made at a friend's expense—

Thus to the finish and this the end :

You lose your portion or lose your friend.

True of the world as of Donegal :

As the brook from the mountain sings to its
    fall

So the drunken man goes down to his fate,

His paunch the coffin of real estate.

Empty the bottle and empty the purse

To the end and certain, bad to worse—

Broad acres your own, grazing and grass—

And are gone in the dregs of the whisky glass.

That man among men I never saw
To add to his store by the aid of the law—
Writ, summons and plea make the lawyers
    fatter,
Who catch their best fish in troubled water.
The fool to its refuge ! The fool is shorn—
Sheep lose their best wool in the sheltering
    thorn.

The House of your Stay it is yours to watch,
For a downdrop creeps through the snuggest
    thatch.
Look not to his faults and forget your own.
For the sin not yours was never known ;
And thin the roofing that does not keep dry
A finger-nail breadth of the meanest sty.

A word in your hearing ! Just listen once more
To the Wit and Wisdom of Rachary Wor.

Three slender things on which all men rest :
The slender stream of milk from the breast,
The slender blade on the green corn-lands,
And the slender thread through the spinner's
    hands.

Three sounds of increase : a lowing cow,
The smithy sparks, the swish of a plough.

Three things strong and a house is blest :
The table, the fire, the hand to a guest.

Three are the tokens of goodly dress :
Elegance, comfort and lastingness.

Three hands and the world its best will yield :
The hand in the smithy, the byre and the field.

Three things to trouble a woman's rest :
A neighbour's butter on bread for a guest,

The word of esteem that comes too slow ;

The washing with never a shirt to show.

Three are the words of grace from the tongue :

The good, the merciful, the word that is sung.

Three sorrowful things for a man of pride :

A saddle but not the horse to ride,

A narrow seat on the country's land,

The treat in the ale-house he cannot stand.

Two have feet that are often bare :

The shoemaker's wife and the smithy mare.

Three are the suits for a man to own :

One for the field where he works his lone,

A second to wear on a market day,

But the best for the church where he goes to

pray.

The Gombeen Man. He is scraggy and thin
And always is getting the money in—
And the money he gathers, penny and pound,
Is fashioned round, but not to go round—
Flat to be built on, and that his say,
As he adds to his portion day and day.
He has rolls of notes and bags of gold,
As much as a wooden chest can hold ;
That he has and nobody knows
What will be done with it when he goes.
But where will he go when he leaves it ?
    Where ?
Nobody knows or seems to care.
Dead, he will count, so good folk tell,
Red-hot coins on the hob of hell.

Three things of wonder I've seen in my day :
The house in which no man kneels to pray,

The thing that feeds fat and is always lean,

The tree that bears where no blossoms have
  been.

Three things of wonder : and these the three :

The grave, the sword and the gallows tree.

Truth has one face, but seven a lie—

All truths are good save three that try :

The truth from the tongue of an angry lass,

The truth that comes from a whisky glass,

And the truth to drive a mother wild,

The ill-timed truth from the lips of her child.

Keep your own guinea. Beware of the friend

Who sleeps while you save but is near when
  you spend.

Share out the loot and finish with blows—

Oh ! who is the soldier whom nobody knows !

Keep to your promise. The world will pay
Heed to " I will " while forgetting " I may."
" I may." To your thatching ! Lone Widow,
    no hope.
" I will." Quick ! The ladder, the straw and
    the rope !

Keep your own counsel. A secret will be
Roared to the world when whispered to three.
" A word in your ear and listen. Speak low !
None know it. 'Twas told me a minute ago."

In the House of the Merry him to the door,
The one who has heard that story before.

On famine your thought when the feasting is
    gay—
Don't cut your scollops on a windy day.

Blessed the Meek who throw aside,

The chains of conceit, the shackles of pride—

Humble, but worthy, as corn is found

When heavy of ear, with its head to the
ground.

Three times married.   Just listen once more

While he speaks of his wives, the Rachary
Wor.

Three things put years on a good man's life :

The curl in the gub of a scolding wife,

The purse in the petticoat he cannot fill

And the nagging tongue that is never still.

In your House be Master.   But remember still,

To a man his due but a woman her will.

So Man of the House be mute in your chair—

Two women and a goose make a noisy fair.

A man in the house and all to himself,
To milk the cows and wash the delf—
The teapot is cold that sits on the hob,
'Tis bad with Herself not there on the job.
A fireless hearth at Wintertide
Is the single man's bed without a bride.

Better to find her, for good or ill.
Across the ditch than across the hill—
And seven leagues is a space to roam,
And I found her there and brought her home—
Oonah from Meenarood, the same
Came into my house and took my name.
Her portion strong. But she loved her gold—
To see was to have and to have was to hold,
And the decency bite folk left on her plate
Was not what they could not but should not
        eat.

What was she not and had she but known,
Better (her talk) to have lived her lone !
Meenarood in her every say,
From the break of dawn to the shut of day—
And soon it was mine to understand
That I married with Oonah her whole townland.

One thing not right ! Another not good !
We did it better at Meenarood !
The milk went thin and the fire went dull :
Just what she expected in Rossnagull !

I can see her now who rests in Heaven,
Seven years my wife, the mother of seven.
Tidy and thrifty she toils and spins
At the shut of day and when day begins :
And the dust she swept from the hearth and floor
Came back in gold to the woman's door.

Near-going Oonah and tight of hand,

And never liked much in her own townland.

Oh ! the back of my hand to her at the door,

Who never adds weight to a poor man's store—

And rusty her heart wherever she lives

Whose eye looks after the gift she gives.

So far so good !   Just listen once more

While he speaks of his second, the Rachary
　　　Wor.

We never see, though we claim to be wise,

The Last Year's snare in the New Year's
　　　guise—

The fair was at Creenan.   I met her there,

The pick of the coolens at Creenan fair

And her face her portion.   But bare, her feet

Never knew the road or the street.

　　c

Her quality style ! Ah there the trouble—
Boots for the cradle—none for the stubble.

Conceited the coolen, cuddled and kissed,
Ring her and then you'll spancell your wrist—
And as woman's warranty set greater store
On the washing tub than the dancing floor.

Discretion her gin. Her blush a lie,
Tricky her heart, fraud in her eye,
Guile in each tress from her curling pins—
Where a man's art finishes a maid's begins.

She would not yesterday ! She will to-day !
Not strange, my son ! 'Tis a woman's way—
As her fishing season has its rise and fall,
Better a sprat than no fish at all

Skittish the woman. Her seed's the same,
For the wild duck's egg is never tame !

Soft are her arms. A hangman's rope
Throttles surer when greased with soap.

Her name was Eileen from Carrigmore.
Dead thirteen years. Her children four.

Three times married. Not me to say
A word of the woman alive to-day.

Over the ditch he has cattle and land—
Oh! big is the crust in the neighbour's hand.
From the start you've striven and striving still!
What road runs straight to the top of the hill?
Bitter your buffets, your stress and strain,
Yet threshing removes the chaff from the grain—
And God, for your work, when he judges that
    same,
Gives so much for the job, but much more for
    the aim.

A moment for thought. Just listen once more
And his talk of Himself—the Rachary Wor.

For seventy years I've lived in peace,
Watching my store and stock increase—
March and mearing stretch far and wide,
Round land the best of the countryside,
Tilth and turbary, meadow and moor—
Prosperous now who once was poor.

And all to what end when my days are told ?
Clay in the face and a bed in the mould
And a prayer maybe, from those who live on
For the Rachary Wor who is dead and gone.

Will I go when the seed is set in the clay
And struggles to rise to the peep of day ?
Or yet when the mowster, sned in hand,
Sweats o'er the swathes in the meadow land ?

Or yet when the brave young eyes alight
Shine to the dance of a Winter night ?

What matters the season ? Where I lie
Will know no change when the Spring goes
    by—
Will know no Spring whose harvest is mown—
Will know no dance of the many I've known—
But this to all :

        Be merciful, kind,
And leave a name that will live behind,
At the certain end all men to bless
The man who is gone, for his righteousness—
And his seed will stand, sound to prevail,
And the name that he leaves will never fail.

And thus his Word, the Rachary Wor,
A man of substance and goodly store—

And he left his holding, his hearth and home

And they buried him deep in the churchyard
 loam.

They carried him there one Lammas-tide,

Thrice seven years now since he died—

But the word that he left will never die

In his own Townland and many forbye,

Where they pray for him still as they did of
 yore,

For the soul of the good man, Rachary Wor.

CHANGELINGS

AND now that I be sittin', it's the neighbours
round to say ;
" He'd a brother and a sister that the fairies
took away,
Round the road and up the hill and down the
hill again
And hid them be the Holy Well that's near the
crooked lane—
Up the lane and down the lane and three times
round the brae,
Niall Beg and Norah Beg the fairies took
away ! "

The pot that's hangin' from the crook is talkin'
    to itself,

Talking to the dresser with the rows of shiny delf,

And up above the chimney brace and hanging
    from the wall

Is the clock that hasn't got a voice and never
    talks at all,

But if it had a voice in it, 'tis up 'twould get
    and say

Where Niall is and Norah is the fairies took
    away.

'Tis nice to live in Dooran now and you so
    very wee,

With a churn for makin' butter and a pot for
    makin' tea—

It's some are great on workin' and some on
    makin' gold—

I'll have a purse and it so full afore I'm very old,

But had I pounds and pounds of gold it's it
    I'd give the day
For Niall Beg and Norah Beg the fairies took
    away.

Now when I'm old and very old, it's out I'll go
    and see
The place that's not for them at all that are
    so very wee—
It's up the hill, across the hill, my bundle in
    my hand,
To travel miles and miles and miles and that
    to Fairyland
And will not tire by light or dark until I meet
    one day
Niall Beg and Norah Beg the fairies took
    away.

TOWNLANDS

Now as townlands these three townlands are
  the best that can be seen,
Meenahalla and Strasallagh and Caghara-
  creen.
Now take the road to Rosses Beag as well as
  Rosses Wor,
And the townlands marching either hand are
  well above a score.

And mark them well in hill and holm, and bog
  and pasture land,
And good strong houses standing snug and
  white on either hand.

42

" Good luck be on ye, decent man ! " The
    girshas passing by
Will have the soft laugh on the lip, the brave
    look in the eye.

The hearty men : " It's warm indeed ! Sit
    down, sir, if you please,
To have a pull iv this old pipe and make
    yourself at ease ! "
" Good bless you, decent man, and all ! " the
    good housewife will say :
" And sit you down and eat a bit to help you
    on the way ! "

And you, out on the Rosses road that runs to
    Rosses Wor,
Will go through many a brave townland and
    they're above a score—

But as townlands these three townlands are
    the best you've ever seen,
Meenahalla and Strasallagh, and Caghara-
    creen !

GREEN RUSHES

It's now for me a petticoat red
And a whip of green rushes,
So out on the road with my eyes ahead
For the lane of the wild thrushes.
Who was it saw my good red dress ?
And who was it saw me dressing ?
'Twas himself indeed and none the less,
And that was a great blessing !

There's many the rush in a whip that's long,
In a whip of green rushes !
There's many a song and them all in song,
In the lane of the wild thrushes.

What wouldn't they give for a petticoat red ?

And wouldn't they call me funny

That's more for the dreams that's filling my
head

Than a crock of good red money ?

THREE ROSES

On her breast were three roses
And she stirred the stirabout pot.
" Where have you got the roses
And are you married or not ? "

The sparks sang up the chimney—
Her brave eyes were so bright.
A pink rose and a red rose
And a rose bog-blossom white.

" Where did I get the roses ?
That's what I'll tell to none,
And how can a girl be married,
And her by herself alone ? "

47

The white neck in my elbow—
The tumbled breasts of desire !
And the roses petal by petal
Dropping into the fire.

The white and the pink and the red rose
Sobbing into the flame—
One couldn't tell where they went to,
One couldn't tell whence they came.

WHEN I WAS WEE

'TWAS me was the divil when I was wee,

Full iv capers and up for fun,

And there wasn't one in the parish like me,

And dear ! how my two bare feet could run

When I was wee !

Fetch or fellow iv me to get

Ye'd wander far on either hand.

But that and all ye'd never set

Eyes on the bate in yer own townland

When I was wee !

Ah ! sharp the tip iv the tongue that's old,

And white the laugh when the lips fall in—

It's the young to laugh and the aged to scold,

The old to pray and the young to sin,

And I was wee.

And ye want to go out to the dance, avic,

As if ye have nothin' else to do ?

And me the poor old man on a stick,

But once I could step on the floor like you

When I was wee !

FISHIN'

Now, who would ye be at the dark iv night
That comes to the door and raps that way,
And fright'nin' me be the fire me lone
And him at his work on Gweebarra Bay,

Fishin' ?

Him at his work and me in the house,
With a league iv water between us two—
Cold and black on me childre dead,
And drowned were the two iv them, Micky and
Hugh,

Fishin'.

It's work for the two iv us ; him at the turf
When the weather is warm, or else the kelp,

And it's knittin' for me, when he bees out
At night on the sea with no one to help,
                                        Fishin'.

'Twas yerself be the door, was it ? All the time !
And, there's fear in yer eyes and yer face is
    white—
Himself it is ! Drowned ! Oh ! Mother iv
    God !
Look down upon me from above this night !
                                    Fishin' !

GARRYBAWN

IT's Micky Eamon Diver and he's only skin
and bone,
With acres holm and heather, that, and money
of his own—
It's all day long he's sitting with his elbow on
the hob,
The crabbit Micky Eamon with his dudheen in
his gob ;
A near old scranny scrape-the-pot that's askin'
dusk and dawn :
" Boy ! are ye never gettin' on with diggin'
Garrybawn ! "

My gallowses are hangin' down and twistin'
    round my legs ;

The girls can see the most of me that's stickin'
    through my rags ;

It's dribs and drabs on back and front and
    freezin' to the pelt—

Ye'll see it's up to him one day and give him
    such a welt !

The close and scringy rip of sin that's at me
    dusk and dawn

With : " Will ye never hurry up with diggin'
    Garrybawn ! "

Now if he's let me to a dance or better to a fair,

A penny whistle I would buy and learn a
    dancin' air—

I'd maybe whistle it at work, or wouldn't it be
    fun

To blow it right in Micky's face at night when
    work bees done !—

It's thrawn he is, the people say, but I can be
    as thrawn—

For Micky Fergus I can't stick, him, and his
    Garrybawn.

But, wait a bit till Old Hall' eve and then you'll
    see my plan ;

It's off from here I'll scoot to where they'll
    treat me like a man,

As good as any in the place, and not because
    I'm wee

They'll curl their gobs and think it smart, that
    looking down on me !

And three pounds comin' ! It's a lot ! Just
    wait till that is drawn

I'll take the road from Micky's house, him, and
    his Garrybawn !

THE WEE MAN

AT night when I be sitting in the corner of the
house,

And oh ! so close and quiet that I wouldn't
scare a mouse,

With the wind above the chimney top and it's
me can hear its song :

" Go to bed you sleepy head, you're staying
up too long ! "

Then Mawmy up and looks at me and says :
" It's now to bed,

Or else 'twill be the Fellow with the Wee Red
Head ! "

Now, sure he's all for capers and up to any
    trick,

It's him to blow the rushlight out and wet the
    candle wick,

It's to a weasel he can turn, for he's the one for
    that,

Or maybe to a clocking hen and maybe to a
    cat—

And things that's worse than that he'll do if
    it's not me in bed—

I'm feeard of him, the Fellow with the Wee
    Red Head !

There's many a thing I'm not to do and that
    because I'm wee,

And if I'm up to any tricks he's got his eye on
    me—

It's him that lets the downdrops in and salts
    the stirabout

And him to shove the kitchen door and give
you such a slout !

Some say the wind is doing it, but don't I know
instead,

It always is the Fellow with the Wee Red Head !

There lives a man across the ditch, a scraggy
man and thin,

But he's the one that has the fist to draw the
money in—

His face that dry and head that bald. He's
only skin and bone,

But that and all though poor he looks, he's
money of his own—

Bags of it and crocks of it, but my ! afore he's
dead,

He'll lose it to the Fellow with the Wee Red
Head.

I'm not a bit afeeard of him and it the light of
    day,

But that is not his time to come and carry boys
    away ;

It's coming down the chimley brace when Maw
    puts out the light,

And round the house and round the house he's
    going all the night—

So now it's me upon my knees and pray and
    then to bed,

Or else 'twill be the Fellow with the Wee Red
    Head !

BREED ASTHOR

Come, cuddle closer, Breed asthor,
For youth will have its way—
The eyes so bright at Candlemas
Grow sad on Lammas Day.

There's bitter bliss in Lammas love
And sure in time to pass,
And wrinkle-rutted dreams of hope
Grow cold at Hallowmass.

Then cuddle closer, Breed asthor,
Ere time brings cark and care ;
We'll catch the fancy born in flame
Ere it goes out in air !

FAIRIES

MEENAHALLA bedding and grass,

Butter and milk in Inishmool,

And big the pastures in Ardnaglass

That has no equal in sheep and wool—

There are seven corners in Donegal,

And acres many meadow and moor ;

Rich in money, but that and all,

The folk of the Rosses are very poor.

The guinea coin is the butt of care,

And hearts are heavy for hands that hold,

But the Rosses people, and they be bare,

Have neither their hearts in gear nor
  gold—

And it's all of them always for song and fun,

First to frolic at dance and spree

With nimble toes when the day is done,

In Carrandooragh and Meenaree.

And they take the gifts from the mill and churn

And the mallard wor on the Rosses bog

To the gentle oak by the Dooran burn

For the little people from Tir nan Og,

Who come with the dusk their gifts to find

In the sacred ring by the haunted oak,

And they weave a spell over souls so kind,

So the Rosses people are happy folk.

FAIRY WORKERS

Said the Fairies of Kilfinnan
To the Fairies of Macroom :
" Oh ! send to us a shuttle
For our little fairy loom,
Our workers, one and twenty
Are waiting in the coom——"
So Kilfinnan got a shuttle
From the Fairies of Macroom.

Kilfinnan got the shuttle,
The shuttle for the loom.
" Now, send us back a hammer,"
Said the Fairies of Macroom.
" We've cobblers, one and twenty,
All idle in their room."

And Kilfinnan sent a hammer
To the Fairies of Macroom.

The Queen of all the Fairies
Sat in her drawing-room :
Her robes came from Kilfinnan
Her brogues came from Macroom.
Now, at the Royal Dinner
The proudest in the room
Were the Fairies from Kilfinnan
And the Fairies from Macroom.

A MOTHER'S TEARS

THERE was a widow and her son.
They lived, the two, in Inishmell—
Her son was bad, and when he died,
St. Peter packed him off to hell.

And in her cabin night and night
When darkness fell and lights were dim
The widow thought upon her son
And wept through all the night for him.

" A mother's love can draw," she said,
" Her children from the deepest sea
But it will never bring my son,
My erring son again to me."

E   65

And saying thus, she wept at dusk,
And saying thus, she wept at dawn,
And then she died.   Her uncle grabbed
Her farm.   His name was Connel Bawn.

She went to Heaven.   There a crowd
Was standing waiting by the gate.
" Now, Widow Bawn," St. Peter said,
" You've caused the crowd, so you must wait."

" I 've caused the crowd ! " said Widow Bawn.
" I do not know what you're about ! "
" Your tears on earth," St. Peter said,
" Have put the Devil's furnace out,

" So we've to house all sinners here
Until the flames of Hell are lit,
For what's the good of souls in Hell
Without a flame to warm the Pit.

" So now it rests with you, Good Soul,

To have the fire relit or drawn."

" Then light it up," the Widow said,

" And keep it hot for Connel Bawn."

THE HERD-BOY

A WEE white cap and a wee green feather—
And who is the chap that's in the heather ?
Speak me the word on the lap of the brae
As the cattle I herd in dusk and the day.

It's nothing I'd doubt of that man of sin
Whose nose sticks out and his chin drops in
And at me all day in the night and the
    morn
With " The cow's in the hay and the stirk's
    in the corn ! "

Then Herself on the ditch bent like a root,
And I know she's a witch hand and foot,

Elbow and shoulder, neck and knee,
With " Ne'er was a bolder rake than me ! "

He's old as the hill, and my ! so thin,
She's older still, all bones and skin !
What they eat when they eat is nothing to see,
And what's left on the plate is left for me !

At school I'm no good.   I'm deaf and I'm dumb,
Can't read a book and can't do a sum !
But leave me my lone on the fields where I
     know
How the birds make the nest and the butter-
     cups grow.

There ! don't you hear it up on the bush !
Watch me go near it.   My ! it's a thrush.
Home of its own in the rowan tree—
It may be its lone but it's not hid from me !

A wee white cap and a wee green feather—
It's me is the chap that's in the heather !
Speak me the word on the lap of the brae
As my cattle I herd in dusk and the day.

THE RETURN

(Argument : Hughie Gallagher, son of the Widow
    Gallagher, returns to Dooran, his native town-
    land with the Fairy Queen his wife.)

WHEN Hughie Gallagher came home, his bosom
    filled with pride,
And brought to Dooran, as his own, his bonnie
    Fairy Bride,
The people gazed on her dismayed.   The
    Widow stroked her chin :
" She's nice enough," the Widow said.   " But
    my ! she's very thin ! "

" Thin's not the word," said Eamon Wor.
    " To meet the work in hand
A ranny like her never yet was seen in all the
    land ;

She's just the woman that meself would never
    want to own.
Thin's not the word," said Eamon Wor.
    " She's only skin and bone."

" More bones than skin," said Norah Friel.
    " Sure, I did never see
A rachary like Hughie's wife, so doncy and so
    wee.
He sure could hide her in his boot or house her
    in his cap !
I never saw a thing like that get married on a
    chap ! "

Said Fergus Dhu who dug for spuds : " God
    help us, but she's small,
The like of her was never seen in County
    Donegal.

The way she walks, the way she talks, her
    figure, cut and shape !
I've hoked up pratees twice as big at Lammas
    on a graip ! "

Neal Hudagh laughed a mighty laugh, as if his
    sides would break—
" Poor Hughie Gallagher," he said. " It's you
    that has the cheek
To take that thing to tend your home. And
    married to her now,
You'll never see her bake or sow, nor churn,
    nor milk a cow."

Said Myles O'Malley : " Grosha Yagh ! that
    such a thing I've seen !
God help you, Hughie Gallagher, you and your
    Fairy Queen !

You've house and home and stock and store,
but all will go to pot,

Because the woman that ye need is what ye
haven't got."

Now Hughie turned him to his wife and looked
at her and said :

" Than house ourselves in Dooran, dear, we'd
better far be dead.

We'll scoot, my love ! " And as he spoke he
caught her by the hand.

And both together toddled off again to Fairy-
land.

THE FAIRY CURSE

THE Carrameera fairies went to Meenawara-
 wor
Where the goodwives placed the butter on the
 lintels of the door—
The fairies went there early before the town
 was up
And every little fairy brought an empty
 buttercup,
But that day they got no butter, for the cats
 were there before,
Cats that licked the fairy lintels o'er in Meena-
 warawor.

Spoke the Queen of all the fairies : " I will
  curse them heart and head,
Curse them in the cradle and curse them in the
  bed,
Curse their stock and substance, curse each
  home and hill,
Curse the hale and hearty and curse the weak
  and ill !
They were happy while they served us, but
  they'll now be sick and sore ! "
This, the curse, the Queen of Fairies put on
  Meenawarawor.

Now all the folk are weeping from the moun-
  tain to the plain,
For the churn that bears no butter and the field
  that bears no grain,

For the fire that will not kindle and the pot
that will not boil,

Since the Fairy Curse is heavy on the shieling,
stock and soil.

Yet the wives still place the butter on the
lintels of the door

And the cats are getting fatter now in Meena-
warawor !

CARRIGDUN

THE good town of Carrigdun has acres hill and
  holm to show,
Turbary upon the moors and corn upon the
  loam to show—
Cows in calf and cows in milk ! See them feed
  together,
On the rich braes of Carridgun their udders on
  the heather !
And foot old Ireland up and down : by hilly
  lands and hollow,
It's Carrigdun to take the lead whatever roads
  you follow !

The good men of Carrigdun are mighty men and
    merry men,

For working and for drinking these good men
    are the very men !

The hardest task in all the land and they're
    the ones to dare it !

The burden that their backs can't bear no
    other backs will bear it !

And models, every man of them of strength,
    grit and sincerity,

As witnesseth their spoken word, their honour
    and prosperity !

The large heart and lavish hand the wives of
    Carrigdun possessed,

And none went hungry in the land, for some to
    all when one possessed,

But none went poor ! For stock and store the
    thrifty wives were rich in—

Butter butts in the pantry stored, sticks of eels
in the kitchen—
And travel left and travel right, and take all
as you find it,
It's Carrigdun a league in front, and other
towns behind it !

The coolens fair of Carrigdun ! Their worth ?
Go, take as token,
The light feet that step a reel ; the strong
hearts hourly broken !
By day beneath the creels of kelp the dear
white feet are moving,
At night—" The night is ours," they say.
" For that's the time for loving."
Come, scrape the fiddle ! Foot the reel ! The
time is now or never !
Bold men, good wives and pretty girls and
Carrigdun for ever !

AT INISHKEEL

House and housing either hand, down here !
Hush you in this calm townland, down here !
There they rest at noon and night,
Twice a spade-length out of sight,

                Down here.

Sleep you all and sleep you well, down here ?
Have you not a word to tell, down here ?
Who have spun and set and sown
In the homes and holms you've known,
Yet you seem to like it well,

                Down here.

Oonah, Norah, Ishabel, down here,
Have you anything to tell, down here ?

Light hands at the spinning wheel,

Feet as light to foot a reel,

Oonah, Norah, Ishabel,

                Down here.

Murtagh, Dermod, Donal Dhu, down here,

Is it well, bold boys, for you, down here ?

At the pattern, dance and fair,

Girls, full-bosomed, miss you there,

And they wait in vain for you

                Down here.

Farley, Peadar, Eamon Wor, down here,

You have neither stock nor store down here.

Heavy-headed corn and rye

Swathe the fields of years gone by,

Farley, Peadar, Eamon Wor,

                Down here.

Tell me, do you like the place, down here ?

Men of mettle, girls of grace, down here ?

Does your heart not long once more

For the fair, the dancing floor ?

Woe and Joy have not a place

                Down here.

House and housing either hand, down here !

Hush you in this calm townland, down here !

Here they rest at noon and night

Twice a spade-length out of sight,

                Down here.

CARRA

IT's back I'd be in my home again, that is up
    by Carra way,
Where quilted petticoats they wear and suits
    of hodden grey,
The good wives by Carra way and bold men
    straight and strong—
And here I walk on grey streets and always
    thinking long !

The whins on flower by Carra way and the lush
    land so still !
And the white lake of Carra sleeps under the
    hush of the hill—

84

Brown loaves in the oven rise, drone the honey
    bees,

The thatched home snug on the braes beneath
    the humming trees !

So it's back I'd be in my home again where
    they wait for me day and day,

In the little house with its hat of thatch that
    stands by Carra way—

Stirabout and buttermilk, a six-hand reel and
    song ;

And here I walk on the grey streets and always
    thinking long !

TWO TOGETHER

CARRICKMACARTH for raking,
Where the good old tales are told !
Greenans for merrymaking
And nobody growing old !
And putting it all together,
If you are the boy for fun,
Minding not wind and weather,
Foot it to Carrigdun !

Now stop on the way a minute
By the marches of Drimagool—
It's land and the cattle in it,
Its mountains white with wool !
And further, by hill and hollow,
Where the burns of white trout run—

Ah ! that is the road to follow,

That takes you to Carrigdun !

When I was supple and hearty,

Fifty years gone by—

Carrickmacarth for a party,

Greenans when blood ran high !

Now, taking the world as you find it,

Say where would the light feet run ?

To a hedge and a girl in behind it !

Ah, young blood and Carrigdun !

BRIAN O'LYNN

(After a Ballad of Merit.)

Brian O'Lynn was a fellow of note ;
He wore a red shirt and he hadn't a coat--
He walked in the rain and the shirt it was thin—
" But it's grand for good weather," said Brian
    O'Lynn.

Brian O'Lynn had a nail in his boot,
And walking the highway, it jagged at his
    foot—
He came to a river ; the boot he threw in.
" Barefooted, no corns," said Brian O'Lynn.

Brian O'Lynn had a master of means,
Who fed the poor servant on pratees and
    beans—

O'Lynn to the threshing, and lay on the bin.

" Empty sacks cannot stand, sir," said Brian
O'Lynn.

Brian O'Lynn regaled at the board ;

With the fat of the townland his stomach was
stored—

He went to the threshing, but would not
begin.

" Full sacks cannot bend, sir," said Brian
O'Lynn.

Brian O'Lynn took Red Ellen for wife ;

A necklace of gold was the wish of her life.

His arms round her neck and he tickled her
chin—

" How's that for a necklace ? " said Brian
O'Lynn.

Brian O'Lynn and his last hour was due.

" Repent or St. Peter will not let you through !"

" I've a trick up my sleeve if he won't let
   me in,

So give me a jemmy," said Brian O'Lynn

TIRCONAIL

Tirconail!

On the hem of the royal Hill, the Hill of
    Aileach,

I stood—

And the Past, the Present and the Future

Were in my eyes

As nothing—

The light foot in a forgotten dance,

A spark in the air.

Tirconail!

Of the dark-haired passes and star-high peaks,

Depths unknown, heights austere,

What have you to say?

What is the message

In the moan of the winds in your glens,

The wail of the waters on your surf-bitten
    shores ?

In the sun-bright lustre of Croagh-an-Airgead,

The haughty coldness of Errigal,

The drum of the sea on Tory,

The white laugh of the waters in Gweebarra
    Bay ?

Errigal has listened to the light feet

On the dancing floors of Gweedore !

Curving and curtseying

The white bones of the time-forgotten dancers

Are one with the waters

That thresh your shores, Tirconail.

For they were and are not,

They are and will not be !

And thus, I, too,

The onlooker of a moment will go.

My moment as nothing,

The strain of a fiddle in the twilight,

A low wind on the hills.

Tirconail !

THE MOTHER

A FULL house when he came
But black with his going !
Tongue of mine gave him name,
My eyes saw him growing !
Not to Mary I'll pray !
Not hers my sorrow.
Can it draw from the spade-deep clay,
My one who is taken away
And rouse him the morrow ?

After the girls, the lad !
The nights he stayed out !
But the dear white body he had
When he was laid out—

And the last dress he wore
On the cold bed lying,
Under the candles four.
And all of them crying,

Norah, Unah and Breed,
Plump girls and hearty—
Didn't they love him indeed !
And me in the party
With not one tear in my eye
For the poor white sleeper.
Ah ! there's blessed ease in a cry,
But my blow struck deeper.

Rootless the young heart's need,
For all their crying—
Norah, Unah and Breed
With strong men lying !
And not to Mary I'll pray !

Not hers my sorrow.

Can it draw from the spade-deep clay,

My one who is taken away

And rouse him the morrow ?

THEY DRANK IN THE TAVERN

THEY drank in the tavern forty years ago,
Farley Og, Shemus Og, Shan and Meehal Roe,
Straight men and strong men, full of fire and
fun,
But now they don't remember them here in
Carrigdun !

The wild herds of Carrigdun loosened for the
fair—
Fit to keep them well in hand the strong men
there.
Wild from the pasturage watch the cattle go,
With Farley Og, Shemus Og, Shan and Meehal
Roe.

G 97

Dressed in your high attire, where do you speed,

Norah and Unah, Eveleen and Breed ?

Breasts of desire, to whom do you go ?

Farley Og, Shemus Og, Shan and Meehal Roe.

And now just as always, the great world rolls
    on—

Fair girls out of sight : strong men gone,

Who drank in the tavern forty years ago,

Farley Og, Shemus Og, Shan and Meehal Roe.

FAIR DREAM

SHE dressed her well in her bodice brown
And well in her gown of gray.
" Off am I to my own love's town
A hundred miles away—
And will not tire by brough or brae
And will walk on the soft-floored sea :
For my love is his from day to day—
But, oh ! does my love love me ?

Has his strong arm a place for my head ?
Will his strong hand feel my breast ?
Fine soft linen and a bridal bed,
For that's what a girl loves best !

99

Word or warning not mine to send

Of the journey so soon to be :

Though my love is his to the world's end.

But, oh ! does my love love me ? "

FAIR LADIES

I PUT an Ant in a Spider's web ;
The Spider, a greedy, grasping sinner,
Collared the Ant for an early dinner,
Forgetting, of course, the Robin's neb !

On the apple-tree Miss Robin sat,
And the morning's tragedy horrified her—
Down she flew and gobbled the Spider,
Forgetting, of course, the watching Cat.

" Mew ! my turn to do my bit,"
Said the Cat, place-proud, benignant, subtle—
Down through the branches shot like a shuttle,
Straight on the Robin and gobbled it.

I know no moral to take from that—

Yet think, a hoary unshriven Sinner,

When I see sweet ladies eating their dinner,

Of the Ant, the Spider, the Robin and Cat.

THE TINKER'S SON

Brogues of buttermilk, petticoats of glass!
Light-footed Unah walks on the grass.
Light-footed Unah from Carrigdun,
Wild in her love for the tinker's son.

Her mother, she stands by the brown half-door.
" A saucy heart," her words, " will soon be
    sore,
For the high step to earth, though high as a
    hill!
But nothing can break a proud girl's will!

" Cows," said the mother. " And seven at
    stake—
The milk they give, and the butter they make!

103

And this to be all for her breed and birth :
A tinker's cart on the roads of the earth !

" And four score sheep stand thick on the
        braes.
Head-high one that another can graze !
And the geese on the holm. Oh, more than one
Has been stuffed in the sack of the tinker's
        son ! "

Brogues of buttermilk, petticoats of glass !
Light-footed Unah walks on the grass.
Light-footed Unah from Carrigdun,
Wild in her love for the tinker's son !

IN THE CROWDED PLACE

In the crowded place
Proudly arrayed—
The look on her face
So little betrayed;
That I watched her passing,
But nothing was said.

In a quiet place
In hodden gray,
They sit at their ease,
Who were young one day!
Would you live and dare it,
Proud Maid, as they?

The loud laugh
Makes for loud crying

Sad the rose

Slow in its dying.

Better its blooms

In the swift wind flying !

In the crowded place

Proudly arrayed.

Would that you were now

In the cold earth laid !

As now, for ever

Be mine, Proud Maid.

And on forever,

If Fates allow

To see you just

As I see you now !

Full-bosomed Maid

With the snow-white brow !

THE CHILDREN'S SONG

THE Wee Red-headed Man is a knowing sort
of fellow.
His coat is cat's-eye green and his pantaloons
are yellow.
His brogues are made of glass and his hose are
red as cherry—
He's the lad for devilment, if you only make
him merry.

He drives a flock of goats, has another flock
behind him—
The little children fear him, but the old folk
never mind him.

To the frogs' house and the goats' house and
    the hilly land and hollow,
He will carry naughty children where their
    parents dare not follow.

Oh ! little ones, beware. If the red-haired man
    should catch you,
Rats will be your playmates and frogs and eels
    will watch you—
A bed between two rocks and not a fire to warm
    you !—
But, little ones, be good and the red-haired man
    can't harm you.

The Wee Red-headed Man has piles and piles
    of riches,
Guineas in his wallet and the pockets of his
    britches,

And if you're very poor and meet him, he is
    willing
To bargain for your soul if you'll sell it for a
    shilling.

He's cute and he is coaxing and hard although
    he's civil—
But let him get your soul and he'll give it to
    the devil,
And when the devil gets it (the devil's hoof is
    cloven)
He'll spit it and he'll steam it and he'll roast
    it in an oven.

But, children, if the Red-haired Man comes up
    to you, don't worry,
Just say, " Excuse me, sir, to-day, for I am in
    a hurry ! "

He'll say, " Be off ! "   Then shake your heels ;

    let one leg race the other

And never turn to look behind, till you get

    home to mother !

IN THE PARISH

MULLANMORE, Meenahalla,
Glenmornan, Strasalla,
By the highway, either hand—
Derrinane, Cornagrilla,
Kilmore, Drimnisilla,
But the best is my own townland !

The strong cows are lowing,
And the prime corn growing,
And heavy the ear of its grain,
Great store of good money,
White trout and wild honey—
And would I were back there again !

111

The big, brown loaves baking—
The fair girls hay-making,
And the cut meadows, swath on sward ;
The flower-bright lane edges,
The haw-speckled hedges
And the fairy raths daisy-starred.

Meenarood and Kilfinnan,
Cleengarra and Crinnan,
That slope to the salt sea strand—
Gortameera, Kingarrow,
Drimeeney, Falcarragh,
But the best is my own townland.

THE DROUTH

A STUMP of a tooth, that was all, in his
  mouth—
A vagabond, always half-dead with the drouth,
Who sober, had little to say.
But give him a drink, and then one would see,
With his pipe in his mouth and his hat on his
  knee,
How he'd talk for a night and a day.

Then : " Once I had stock and once I had
  store,
A house of my own and prime cattle galore,
A table and dresser and delf.

And the best of the country sat down at my
    board,
Fed full and hearty and thanking the Lord,
In the very same voice, thanked myself.

" Invited to parties ! Aye, always the first,
Till the neighbours grew sick of my damnable
    thirst
And shut their black doors in my face !
Then to add to my sorrows the bailiffs came
    round,
Put my acres to auction, my beasts to the
    pound,
And now—neither penny nor place !

Four score his years. Half-dead with the
    drouth,
Porter he'd drink through a clay-crusted clout,

But sober he's nothing to say.

But give him a deoch if you've porter to spare,

And see him sit down at his ease on a chair,

And he'll speak for a night and a day.

NIGHT

(She, who sits in the Lamplight and whose Shadow
is thrown on the red window Blind, is the Speaker.)

AND what do ye want at all, at all ?

And what do ye want at all ?

Raking about at the shut of day,

With yer own townland three miles away ?

Three long miles to have put behind,

To look from the dark through an old red blind !

So what do ye want at all ?

(He, who, for an hour has been exploring the Blind
to find a crack to peep through, is the Speaker.)

And what do I want at all, at all,

And what do I want at all ?

Three hard miles I won't do again

To flatten my nose on an icy pane—

And ye, sittin' snug at the back of the blind,

That hasn't the go to make up yer mind

To come out for a minute at all !

(Two are speaking in the darkness. Whispers,
kisses, protestations, reproofs, etc. One Listener
unseen hears all, a Wren who shelters in the hedge-
row. This the Conversation as the Wren hears it.)

And what do ye want at all, at all ?—

And what do ye want at all ?—

Takin' me out on a night like this !—

Now, will ye ?—I won't ! Another wee kiss !—

Oh ! the boys that are here about nowadays !—

And the girls that are and so hard to plase !—

BUT WE'RE HAPPY ENOUGH AND ALL !

THE DARK BLOSSOM

To market ; her feet on the hard road—
Not hard as the heart within her !
To Mass : and her dark sins a load—
The dark and dear little sinner !
What will I do with myself
Day and daily ?
Proud you grow while I grow thin,
Hard heart and soul of sin,
Eileen Faly !

GIRLS

WHERE they walk along on the green :
Their white feet,
The lilt of a song and their teeth are seen
Like white stones,
Little white stones
In the pink of the dawn !

Have you seen them at all
On the green grass ?
The white feet that softly pass
On the sod ?
And the dews of God
Hang as they hung

On the heather, the flowers and the grass

Where their feet have trod !

Silk-soft, milk-white,

The feet are moving,

The air of a song—a forgotten song

That seeks its words,

The lost white feathers

Of holy birds.

SLAN LEATH

ONCE 'twas my song at a ball,
My dance at a wedding,
But now the bones of me call
For bed and bedding,
Sheet and sheeting that's sound,
And I will go off in
Pomp to the house in the ground,
The clay in a coffin.

'Tis seed-time at Candlemas,
Then, there let it !
There are, when I come to pass,
Fine men to set it,

Men and them hale and strong—
Of breed and breeding.
Their hands won't idle long,
Sowing and seeding !

It's a brave turf fire the night
In the house I've grown old in—
A narrow home is in sight,
But room to grow cold in !
Is it Candlemas now with its rain ?
Or Lammas Day with the mowing ?
Neither will know me again,
And it time to be going.

SONGS

OF

THE DEAD END

PATRICK MacGILL was born at Glenties, a little village in one of the wildest districts of Donegal on the north coast of Ireland, twenty-one years ago. The eldest of a family of ten, he had to go out into the world at a very early age and begin his fight in the great battle of life. When twelve years old he was engaged as a farm hand in the Irish Midlands, where his day's work began at five o'clock in the morning and went on till eleven at night through Summer and Winter. It was a man's work with a boy's pay. At fourteen, seeking newer fields, he crossed from 'Derry to Scotland; and there for seven years was either a farm hand, drainer, tramp, hammerman, navvy, plate-layer or wrestler. During all these years he devoted part of his spare time to reading, and found relief from the drag of the twelve-hour shift in the companionship of books. At nineteen he published " Gleanings from a Navvy's Scrap-book," of which 8000 copies were sold. Encouraged by the success which marked this venture, he immediately gathered material for a new volume, and while engaged in so doing, received an appointment on the editorial staff of the " Daily Express," and in September, 1911, left the service of the Caledonian Railway Company at Greenock and came to London. In the following year he relinquished his post with the newspaper, and published " Songs of a Navvy." This, as well as the former, being now out of print, he has put together some of the pieces out of either, re-written others, and added fresh ones to the same in the present *" Songs of the Dead End."*

J. N. D.

WINDSOR, July, 1912

THE NAVVY

REMOTE from mansion and from mart,
    Beyond our outer, furrowed fields —
One with the rock he cleaves apart,
    One with the weary pick he wields —
Bowed with his weight of discontent,
    Beneath the heavens sagging gray,
His steaming shoulders stark and bent,
    He drags his joyless years away.

For dreamy dames with haughty eyes,
    And cunning men with soft white hands
Have offered you in sacrifice
    Lone outcast of the outcast lands.
For all the furs that keep them warm,
    For all the food that keeps them fit,
Through all the years they 've wrought you harm,
    And take a churlish pride in it.

Brutish we 've hashed it far and near,
    I 've shared your woe and dull despair;
We 've sung our songs, and none to hear,
    And told our wrongs, and none to care.
Some day — how soon we may not tell —
    We 'll rend the riven fetters free.
Till then, may heaven guard you well,
    And God be good to you — and me.

CONTENTS

I do not sing
 Of angel fair or damozel
  That leans athwart a painted sky;
 My little verses only tell
  How human beings live and die,
  And labour as their years go by.

I do not sing
 Of plaster saints or jealous gods,
  But of the little ones I know,
 Who paint their cheeks or bear their hods
  Because they live in doing so
  Their hapless life on earth below.

I sing of them
 Whose lives are varied as their creeds —
  I've shared their every toil and care,
 I know their many hopes and needs,
  I've seen Death take them unaware;
  Mayhap some day their death I'll share.

I sing their life,
 Misknown, miscalled, misunderstood,
  Its ups and downs, its outs and ins;
 I know the evil and the good,
  Where virtue ends and vice begins —
  But judge no mortal by his sins.

I sing of them,
 The underworld, the great oppressed,
  Befooled of parson, priest, and king,
 Who mutely plod earth's pregnant breast,
  Who weary of their sorrowing,
  — The Great Unwashed — of them I sing.

I sing my songs,
 In mirthful guise or woeful strain;
  I've dwelt where woe and hunger dwell,
 And told my rosaries of pain —
  I sing my songs to you — and well,
  You'll maybe like them — who can tell?

1911

THESE VERSES ARE DEDICATED

TO

My Pick and Shovel

Because we have swined in the drift,
  Because we have horsed it alone,
Strong, unafraid, or in shine or in shade,
  Companionless and unknown ;

Because we have laboured our bit
  For all our impetuous worth,
Roughing it hard, discarded and scarred,
  In the uttermost corners of earth ;

Through the drag of the long, stagnant day,
  Where the infinite wilderness is,
As we slunk from the breath of an imminent death
  In this tortuous world of His ;

Since we have been pals of the wild,
  Tried in the furnace and true,
Don't take it amiss if I dedicate this
  Volume of verses to you.

PATRICK MACGILL.

ON THE OPEN ROAD,
  October, 1911

Songs of the Dead End

THE PICK

IN the depths of the pluvial season it gallantly stayed
    to your hand,
In the dead end of woe and creation, afar in the fur-
    thermost land,
When the saturnine heavens hung o'er you as dark as
    the ultimate tomb,
When the trough of the valley you gutted was filled
    with ineffable gloom,
When down in the depths of the planet uprooting the
    brontosaur's bed,
With the fire damp writhing around you, and a candle
    affixed to your head,
When the gold-seeking fever enthralled you, when you
    fitfully watered the pan,
Ever it strove to your bidding, ever it aided your plan,
Ready, resistless, reticent, friend of the conquering man!

See that its edge is like silver, tempered to try and be
    tried,
Look on your pick as a lover would gaze on the girl
    at his side,
If it responds to your promptings, when the navvy men
    hurry and sweat,
If it be proof to the tempest, when the clouds and the
    dirt-bed have met,
If its handle be graceful and lissome, slipping and soft
    in the hand,

Brothers, 't is meet for its mission, tend it, for ye under-
stand;
Try it with fire and with water, try it in sand and in
rock,
See that the slag can't resist it, see that it beareth the
shock,
Hurling the rock from its fastness, goring the destitute
earth,
Tearing the guts of the tunnel, seeking the coal for the
hearth
Down in the stygian darkness, ye who can reckon its
worth!

Work it for days one and twenty, then if it 's true to
the test,
Look on your pick as a maiden, but often the pick is
the best,
For the temper of women when broken, e'en heaven
can't better the same,
But the pick will regain what it loses with the touch
of the hammer and flame,
And for aye will it answer your yearning, be true to
the trust that ye place,
But ofttimes the falsest of females is fair in the glance of
the face,
And fickle, and sure as she 's fickle, your sweetheart in
labour is true
As long as there 's grub on the hot-plate, as long as
there 's hashing to do,
While the hail-harried winter is scowling, while the
skies of the summer are blue.

Enough! for the pick has been trusted, enough! for the
pick has been tried

In the uncharted lands of the world, past where the
pathways divide,
Where the many lead into the city of mimicry, aping
and show,
Where one leads away to the vastness, the infinite vast-
ness you know,
And there with the grim pioneer it wrought in the
shine and the shade,
While he feared in the gloom and the silence, afraid as
a child is afraid,
Pleased with his rough hand's caresses, slave to his
wish and his whim —
Away on the fringe of the world, comrade and
brother to him.

Enough, for the pick has been trusted, in hazardous,
desperate years,
When the wine press was trodden alone for the vintage
of sorrow and tears,
Under the blight of the upas, the bane of the vampire's
wing,
Shaping the founds of a temple, razing the keeps of a
king;
To labour that stood as its sponsor for the fiery baptism
given,
It has proved its worth, on a toil-curséd earth, and
under the eyes of heaven;
Staunch in the pitiless combat, vigorous, virile and bold,
To-day I give it the honour our fathers denied it of
old,
To-day I have sung its praises, and told of the honour
due
To the pick that was ever trusted, tried on the dead-
line and true.

THE SONG OF THE SHOVEL

DOWN on creation's muck-pile where the sinful
swelter and sweat,
Where the scum of the earth foregather, rough and un-
tutored yet,
Where they swear in the six-foot spaces, or toil in the
barrow squad,
The men of unshaven faces, the ranks of the very bad;
Where the brute is more than the human, the muscle
more than the mind,
Where their gods are the loud-voiced gaffers, rugged,
uncouth, unkind;
Where the rough of the road are roosting, where the
failed and the fallen be,
There have we met in the ditchway, there have I
plighted with thee,
The wage-slave troth of our union, and found thee true
to my trust,
Stoic in loveless labour, companion when beggared and
burst,
Wonderful navvy shovel, last of tools and the first.

Your grace is the grace of a woman, you're strong as
the oak is strong;
Wonderful unto the navvy, the navvy who sings your
song —
For ever patient, and ready to do what your master bids,
Though you laboured at Beni Hassan, and wrought at
the Pyramids,
Uprearing the Grecian temple, the gold Byzantium
dome,

The palaces proud of Susa, the legended walls of
  Rome,
In the earliest days of Egypt, in evil-starred Nineveh,
When your masters who be were whirling, inane in the
  Milky Way,
In Pompeii of the sorrows, ere the lava of hate was
  hurled
From the fiery mouth of the mountain, in the passionate
  days of the world.

Older than all tradition, older than Ops or Thor,
Gods of the Dane or Roman, gods of the plough or
  war,
In dark preadamite ages used by the primitive
  man,
And unto his needs were shapen ere custom and cant
  began —
A servant to Talos the Potter were you in the ages
  dim —
But you helped in the drift of seasons to fashion the
  urn for him.

But you 're foul to the haughty woman, bediamonded
  slave of lust,
Who bows to a seignior's sabre, tinged with a coward's
  rust,
Foul to the aping dandy with the glittering finger
  rings,
You who have helped to fashion the charnel vault of
  the kings!
— Ah! the lady fair is disdainful and loathingly looks
  askew,
And the collared ass of the circle gazes in scorn at
  you,

But some day you 'll scatter the clay on grinning lady
and lord,
For yours is the cynical triumph over the sceptre and
sword!

Emperors pass in an hour, empires pass in a day,
But you of the line and muckpile open the grave
alway.

Tell me what are thy graces, what are the merits of
thine?
Answer ye slaves of the railway, answer ye dupes of
the mine.
What do you mean to the navvy, moleskinned serf of
the ditch,
Piling the courts of pleasure up for the vampire rich?
What do you mean to the muck-men, forespent slaves
of the street?
Life for the wives that love them, food for their babes
to eat,
Who wear their fetters of being, down where no sun-
shine comes
In the Christian country of sorrows, the civilized land
of slums.

Wonderful, ancient shovel, tool of the labour slave!
To you the sparkle of silver the hammer and furnace
gave,
For you the virginal forest was stripped of its stateliest
trees,
And you have the temper that flame has, and you have
the graces of these.
Athens and Rome have known you, London and Paris
know.

You'll raise the towns of the future when the towns
  of the present go —
A race will esteem and praise you in the days that are
  to be,
When I am silent and songless and the headstone crum-
  bles on me!

Wonderful navvy shovel, the days are near at hand
When you'll rise o'er sword and sceptre a mighty
    power in the land.

B

BY–THE–WAY

THESE be the little verses, rough and uncultured, which
I 've written in hut and model, deep in the dirty ditch,
On the upturned hod by the palace made for the idle rich.

Out on the happy highway, or lines where the engines go,
Which fact you may hardly credit, still for your doubts 'tis so,
For I am the person who wrote them, and surely to God, I know!

Wrote them beside the hot-plate, or under the chilling skies,
Some of them true as death is, some of them merely lies,
Some of them very foolish, some of them otherwise.

Little sorrows and hopings, little and rugged Rhymes,
Some of them maybe distasteful to the moral men of our times,
Some of them marked against me in the Book of the Many Crimes.

These, the Songs of a Navvy, bearing the taint of the brute,
Unasked, uncouth, unworthy, out to the world I put,
Stamped with the brand of labour, the heel of a navvy's boot.

A NAVVY'S PHILOSOPHY

A CROSS life's varied ways we drift
Unto the tomb that yawns in wait,
One ruling o'er the mighty state,
One sweating on the double shift.

I 've whirled adown the sinful slope
That leads to chasms of despair,
And dwelt in haunts of hunger where
The spectre sorrow jeers at hope.

My ways are cast with many men
Who fight with destiny and fail,
The down and outers of the jail,
The tavern and the gambling den —

The men who bet and drink and curse,
Who tread the labyrinthine maze
Of sin, who move on rugged ways,
Who might be better — ay, and worse!

My dead-end comrades true as steel,
The men who bravely bear the goad,
The wild uncultured of the road —
Like them I speak just as I feel.

'Neath silver skies with silence shod,
Engirdled by the Milky Way,
And set with stars of brightest ray,
As fits the far-off paths of God,

I 've slept with them; in lonely lands,
    Ere came the city vomit thence
    To take the house and claim the fence
Built with the toil of calloused hands,

I 've wrought with them; where gin shops smell,
    And stagnant models smut the town,
    I 've shared their plaints when out and down —
My brothers, don't I know them well!

I 've begged with them from door to door,
    And thought unutterable things
    Of lands where courtiers and where kings
Still grind the ʿaces of the poor.

   .   .   .   .

The cold grub eaten in the dawn,
    The wet shag smouldering as you smoke,
    For ever being down and broke,
You learn to like it — later on.

You learn to like it — for you must,
    Though hardly worth the pains you take,
    Or yet the sacrifice you make —
The barter for the vital crust.

Of things abstruse I cannot sing
    In fitting strains, so let me say,
    From hand to mouth, from day to day
Is not the right and proper thing.

   .   .   .   .

But let me sing in gayer strain,
    The glory of the wilder life,
    Apart a little from the strife,
The feline fury and the pain.

Despite the hate insensate which
  The fates have borne to crush me low,
  I love to watch the puppet show
And count myself exceeding rich.

You say I own no lordly halls,
  No parks extending far and wide,
  No cornice, column, cusp of pride,
No paintings hanging from my walls.

No hall of pride with fresco decked —?
  My mountain pillars rear on high,
  My floor the earth, my roof the sky,
And God Himself the Architect.

No paintings from a master's hand —?
  My canvas spreads from flower to star
  Barbaric, grand, anear, afar,
From sea to sea, from land to land.

No deep cathedral music swells
  For me, you say, I own it true,
  But under Heaven's gentian blue,
What strains of sweetness fill the dells!

The rustle of the wind-swept trees,
  The robin's song at early morn,
  The larks above the crimson corn,
What music in the world like these!

All, all are mine. The simple flower,
  The ocean in its madding wrath,
  The drunken wind that beats my path,
The arched skies that shine or lower.

I 've sailed on ships with sails of fire,
  By amber ports, through carmine seas,
  And opal-tinted argosies,
To dreamt-of islands of desire.

For me the music of the streams,
  The tints of gold on heath and furze,
  Where wind-blown gorse clumps shake their spurs,
For me the wonder-world of dreams.

While you are selling at the mart,
  Or buying souls to glut your greed,
  (Who fatten on your brother's need,)
In lonely ways I dwell apart:

Or when the jewelled carcanet
  Of Heaven decks the darkling sky,
  Beside the cabin fire I lie
And smoke my soothing cigarette,

And dip in some enchanted page,
  Or linger o'er a story told
  By some grey chronicler of old,
The dreamer of a long-past age.

And as the smoke wreaths rise, meseems
  I live in Ind or Babylon,
  And share the hopes of poets gone,
The dreamers of æsthetic dreams.

Or sing of Rome, or bleed for Troy,
  Or dwell in Tyre or Nineveh —
  But ah! 'tis fancy's boundless play,
The wayward dreamings of a boy.

'Tis sweet to write it down in verse,
  Or think of it, but all the same,
  If e'er you try you'll find the game
Is hardly worth a tinker's curse.

The open road is passing grand
  When skimming on a motor car,
  But dossing 'neath the pallid star
Is something you don't understand.

In fact you'll hardly realize
  While lounging in your drawing room,
  How drear December's dirge of doom
Across the snow-clad level flies.

Or how the frosty crowbar sears
  The hand that lifts it from the drift —
  You'll learn it on the ten-hour shift
Where I was learning all these years.

You'll likewise learn the useful rule,
  The motto of the navvy man,
  To do as little as you can
And keep your pipe and stomach full.

The song I sing is very rude,
  In sin mayhap my life I live,
  But ye are wise and will forgive
As none of us are very good.

We sin — we'll sorrow later on!
  We laugh — some day we're sure to weep!
  We live — by night we'll fall asleep,
And none may waken us at dawn!

And we are brothers one and all,
 Some day we 'll know through Heaven's grace,
 And then the drudge will find a place
Beside the master of the hall.

THE FAITH OF A CHILD

I 'VE learned the tale of the crooning waves
　　And the lore of the honey bee,
The Mermaids' song in the lonely caves
　　Of Rosses by the sea.

For I 'm never let out to the dance and wake,
　　Because I 'm a gasair small;
But stay at home, for my mother's sake,
　　And never grow weary at all.

She taught me the lore of the fairy men,
　　Who live in the haunted rath;
And tells me to pray to Mary, when
　　I cross the gossamer path.

For it 's true that the gossamer threads are thrown
　　From the holly tree to the grass,
When the moon-white night is long and lone,
　　For the fairy band to pass.

But, if ever you cross their way at all,
　　May Mary be with you then,
For they steal the children into their hall
　　That 's hid in the haunted glen.

The hall that 's under the gentle thorn,
　　Where my little brother must stay,
For the fairies came, before I was born,
　　And stole my brother away.

And mother says he is free from pain
    (They have kept him seven years)
Yet she 'd rather far have him back again,
    And tells me so in tears.

Ah! many a song she has sung to me,
    And many a song she knew,
And many a story there used to be,
    And Mother's tales are true.

So I know the chant of the crooning waves
    And the lore of the honey bee,
And the Mermaids' song in the lonely caves,
    Of Rosses by the sea.

FISHING

WHEN the sheep on the brae are lying still
　　And the lone lake waters weep,
When the pale-faced moon comes over the hill
　　And my brothers and sisters sleep,
I wander out by the brooklet's edge
　　Where moon-limned waters run,
And see the fays from the trailing sedge
　　Come silently one by one —

Come silently out to fish for trout
　　With a hook of silver fine,
A rye-grass stalk for a fishing-rod,
　　And a gossamer thread for line.

But there isn't a fish in all the brook,
　　And it's me that ought to know,
For I caught the little minnows and took
　　Them with me long ago —
I lifted them up from the golden sand
　　Into my pannikin small,
Yet the fairies stay till the dawn of day
　　And never catch one at all.

I took the little minnows myself
　　And left them down in the well,
As nobody saw me place them there,
　　Sure no one at all can tell
The fairy fishers where they are gone,
　　The pretty wee fish inside
The well that is marked by St. Colum's cross
　　And the cross of good Saint Bride!

THE SONG OF THE TRAMPS

THE eager hands will never take us back,
    The luring eyes will never draw us home,
With the changing heaven o'er us, and the white road
      stretched before us,
    Sure the world is ours to revel in and roam —
    We have padded it, alone, afar, apart,
    We have roughed it to the ultimate extremes,
Where the blazing dawn-tints kindle, or the sun-kissed
      rivers dwindle
    In a land of fairy fantasies and dreams.

    Would we linger in the city and the stench,
    The alleys and the fetid walls amid,
In the dirt beyond all telling of the festered, filthy
      dwelling
    And the gutter degradation — God forbid!
    We are not the fools you reckon us to be,
    Our woebegone appearances are shammed,
Tho' we act the discontented, on the byways unfre-
      quented,
    We are n't so incorrigibly damned.

    We doss it 'neath the timid shaky stars,
    Where the mountains shrink and cower overawed,
In the gaunt mysterious places, with the dew upon our
      faces,
    While the breathless night goes by in silence shod,
    As the pallid, leprous, moon above us frets,
    By the fitful fire-flames flickering undersized,
We think as men unshriven, of an evil unforgiven,
    Of the many hopes we never realized.

Oh! the dreaming and the fancy and the hope,
The wonder and the worry of it all,
The gipsy blood that's flowing through our veins will
   keep us going
   On the road while thrushes sing or sparrows fall;
By meadows waving lazily and slow,
By streamlets singing songs of wild desires,
And the eyes of heaven peeping will keep watch above
   us sleeping,
   And the dawn will see the ashes of our fires.

To the wealth of Mother Nature we are heirs,
The skies of opal, amber, sapphire hue,
The moorland and the meadows, the sunshine and the
   shadows,
   We love them — for we've nothing else to do!
The eager hands will never lure us back,
The plaintive eyes can never draw us home,
With the heaven bending o'er us and the white road
   stretched before us,
   Sure the world is ours to revel in and roam.

THE SONG OF THE LOST

WHAT will be left when the siren city
    Ceases to lure and ceases to pay,
When poverty hovers across my way,
When years have sullied my sinful grace?
No mother's love, and no father's pity,
No fondling lover, no children gay,
To plant a kiss on their mother's face.

The kisses I 've had were born of passion,
And the love was the lust of brutal men
Wild from the bar or gambling den,
My jewels were bought in a soul's eclipse,
For I was gay in an evil fashion —
Queen of the sodden alley, when
They paid for kissing my painted lips.

Look how the lamps of London twinkle,
Hark how the bells of London toll,
" Pledge thyself for the devil's dole,
Fool of the empty tinsel show —
But what avails when the brow shall wrinkle,
The lone regrets of a stricken soul,
The nightly wail of a sleepless woe? "

FATE

THE cloudwrack o'er the heaven flies,
   The wild wind whistles on the lake,
   The drooping branches in the brake
Mourn for the pale blue butterflies.

Where is the sheen of green and gold?
   The sullen Winter's beard is hoar.
   Where are the fruits the Autumn bore?
We know not, who are growing old.

We pulled the dainty flowers of spring,
   But we were happy being young —
   And now when Autumn's knell is rung
We wither 'neath the vampire wing.

THE BOOTLESS BAIRN

(1909)

DAYS of the whirling snowflakes, nights of the
        weeping wind,
That move to a gloomy future, that come from the
        dark behind,
Carry upon their bosoms the sorrows of hope defiled —
The wail of the bootless bairn, the cry of the hapless
        child.

Not for him is the Christmas and all the sweets it
        brings,
Nor does he share the New Year's hope of bright and
        beautiful things,
Ah, never for him is the festal board with Nature's
        bounties piled,
The wan-eyed bootless bairn — the poor, uncared-for
        child.

Oh! why do we prate of our glory and lightning let-
        tered fame,
When the winds of the city roadways are breathing
        our people's shame?
And ev'ry castle builded is a hundred homes despoiled —
Our fame leaves the bairn bootless, our glory the hap-
        less child.

Then it is ours to labour and help with the passing
        suns,
To brighten with word and action the lot of the little
        ones,
For the sins of our age hang heavy on defiler and defiled,
They fall on the bootless bairn, and crush the hapless child.

THE SONG OF THE CIGARETTE

(1908)

There with a Book of verse beneath the Bough,
A Flask of Wine, a Loaf of Bread, and Thou,
My Woodbine Packet in the Wilderness —
And Wilderness is Paradise enow.

— OMAR KHAYYAM
(*As he would write to-day.*)

GET thee gone, my erstwhile loved one, I am weary
of your sighs,
Smothered by your fond embraces, tired gazing in your
eyes —
No, I do not want to nurse him — Baby, prattling
little fool —
Would he were a little older, we would pack him off
to school —
No, confound the morning paper, take it from the
blessed room,
I am sick of Peer-less Asquith, Crippen, and the Rub-
ber Boom.
Now the cosy room is quiet, and I hope the world
will let
Me sit down in calm enjoyment to my soothing
cigarette.

Let me see what brand will suit me; ah, it does n't
matter much,
Every cigarette 's a pleasure, so I 'll take one up as
such;
Oh, the delicate aroma! What perfume could e'er
excel?
Oh, the beautiful tobacco and the life-inspiring smell.

c

What is wine, and what is woman? Vanity, the
      preacher says,
If there 's vanity in smoking, I am vain for all my
      days.
Slightly changed, what says my Kipling? Recollect
      'tis not a joke,
What 's a woman? Just a woman, but — a cigarette 's
      a smoke.

England 's kicking up a racket on the passing of the
      Peers.
Let them pass, I care not twopence while this smoke
      goes past my ears;
What the mischief am I caring if the German army
      comes,
I will smoke in peace and paper 'mid the rolling of
      their drums;

Let them fly until they 're stupid, man was ever vain,
      I know,
Why the reptiles (Latin something) flew ten thousand
      years ago!
All the world 's a show of puppets, and the wisest of
      them yet
Sits behind the scenes and calmly smokes a Woodbine
      cigarette.

Let the sickly poet picture scenes from his excited mind,
If I 'm left unto my smoking then the gods are very
      kind;
Let the taxing legislators tax the beer and all the rest,
If they spare my gentle Lady then I 'm very surely
      blest;
Makers of the law and sufferers, mankind of whatever
      stamp,

Prince or pauper, saint or sinner, tyrant, teacher,
   tailor, tramp,
Leave me, and I ask for little, but that little I must
   get,
Just a cosy spot and silence and a soothing cigarette.

THE SLUM-CHILD

(1909)

THERE is meeting and parting
    The wide world over,
      Day by day,
Of true hearts and fond hearts,
    The maid and the lover,
      And thus alway.

But never a parting
    Will give me sorrow,
      And never comes
The hope of the friends
    I 'll meet to-morrow —
      I 'm of the slums.

Day and night are forever
    So dreary:
      I never know
Aught of a friend,
    When the heart is weary
      To let him know.

But often I pray when the
    Night is gloomy,
      That God would send,
In all His mercy, from
    Heaven to me,
      One loving friend.

IN THE MIDNIGHT

A SPLASH on the dusky water,
    A cry on the winter air,
As from the pit abyssmal
    Rises a soul's despair.

The human ghouls of midnight
    Shiver beneath the snow,
The painted women in terror
    Stand, and listen, and — go.

Up in the deep of heaven,
    Gloomy and ghostly grey,
The cry of the lost one falters —
    Falters, and dies away.

Only a cry in the darkness,
    Only a swirl in the tide,
Only a sinful woman
    Crossing the Great Divide!

THE CALLING VOICE

THE great world voice is calling, and the streams
    have lost their glory,
    For their restless waters journey to the ever-moving
    sea,
And I am ever yearning as they seem to breathe a story
    Of the better things to be, the better things to be.

The breeze is saying, " Hasten, we will cross the seas
    together,
    You and I together to a fairer world than this,
Say, does the mountain keep you and the purple waving
    heather,
    Or the little girl you kiss, the little girl you kiss? "

No more the valley charms me, and no more the tor-
    rents glisten,
    My love is plain and homely, and my thoughts are
    far away,
The great world voice is calling, and with throbbing
    heart I listen,
    And I cannot but obey, I cannot but obey.

ROAMING

I STEADY my staff at the crossroads, it falls with
the breeze from the south,
I hie to the northern meadows with the kiss of the
morn on my mouth,
The dawn is of opal and ruby, the dew glitters soft on
my breast,
And the road lies away o'er the world, and the life of
the road is the best.

The gossamer lies on the greensward like threads made
of silvery fire,
And the breeze in the hedgerows is singing like strains
of a magical lyre;
There is lure in the woods of the east-land, and health
in the fields of the west,
And the road lieth over the world, and the life of the
road is the best.

I steady my staff at the crossroads, it speaks of a south-
ern land
In the winning and wonderful language the staff and
myself understand,
For wherever it falls I will follow, nor question its
loving behest,
For the road runs the wide world over, and the life of
the road is the best.

PADDING IT

An empty stomach, an empty sack and a long road.
                                            — From Moleskin's Diary.

HASHING it out like niggers on a two and a
     tanner sub,
Everything sunk with our uncle, little to burn at the
     pub,
Fifty and six were our hours, and never an extra shift,
And whiles we were plunging at banker, and whiles we
     were studying thrift —
Sewing and patching the trousers, till their parts were
     more than the whole,
Tailoring, cobbling, and darning, grubbed on a sausage
     and roll —
Thrift on a fourpenny hour, a matter of nineteen bob,
But we glanced askew at the gaffer, and stuck like glue
     to the job,
We of the soapless legion, we of the hammer and hod,
Human swine of the muck-pile, forever forgotten of
     God.

" Hearing of anything better ? " one to another would
     say,
As we toiled in all moods of the weather, and cursed at
     the dragging day,
Winking the sweat off our lashes, shaking the wet off
     our hair,
Wishing to God it was raining, praying to Him it
     would fair.

"Curse a job in the country," one unto one would
    reply,
Looking across his shoulder, to see if the boss was by —
Arrogant March came roaring down on the year, and
    then
A rumour spread in the model, and gladdened the
    navvy men.

Was it the highland slogan? was it the bird of the
    north,
Out of its frost-rimmed eyrie that carried the message
    forth?
"Jackson has need of navvies, the navvies who under-
    stand
The graft of the offside reaches, to labour where God
    has bann'd,
Men of the sign of the moleskin who swear by the
    soundless pit,
Men who are eager for money and hurry in spending it.
Bluchers and velvet waistcoats, and kneestraps below
    their knees,
The great unwashed of the model — Jackson has need
    of these."

Then the labourer on the railway laughed at the en-
    gine peals,
And threw his outworn shovel beneath the flange of the
    wheels.
The hammerman at the jumper slung his hammer
    aside,
Lifted his lying money and silently did a slide,
The hod was thrown on the mortar, the spade was
    flung in the drain,
The grub was left on the hot-plate, and the navvies
    were out again.

All the roads of the Kingdom converged, as it were, to
    one.
Which led away to the northward under the dusk and
    dawn,
And out on the road we hurried, rugous and worn and
    thin,
Our cracking joints a-staring out through our parch-
    ment skin,
Some of us trained from our childhood, to swab in the
    slush and muck,
Some who were new to the shovel, some who were
    down on their luck,
The prodigal son half home-sick, the jail-bird, dodger
    and thief,
The chucker-out from the gin shop, the lawyer minus a
    brief,
The green hand over from Oir'lan', the sailor tired of
    his ships,
Some with hair of silver, some with a woman's lips,
Old, anæmic, and bilious, lusty, lanky and slim,
Padding it, slowly and surely, padding it resolute, grim.

We dossed it under the heavens, watching the moon
    ashine,
And a tremor akin to palsy quivering down the spine.
We drank of the spring by the roadside using the hands
    for a cup,
Stole the fowl from the farm before the farmer was up,
We lit our fires in the darkness drumming up in the
    flame,
Primitive, rude, romantic men who were old at the
    game,
On through the palpable darkness, and on through the
    tinted dawn,
The line of moleskin and leather fitfully plodded on;

And no one faltered or weakened, and no one stumbled
    or fell,
But now and again they grumbled, saying, " It 's worse
    nor hell."
The rain came splattering earthwards, slavering in our
    face,
But we never hinted of shelter and never slackened our
    pace,
The mornings were cool and lightsome, we never hur-
    ried a bit,
" Slow and easy is better than hashing and rushing it."
Ever the self-same logic, steady, sober and suave —
" The hasty horse will stumble," " hashing to make
    your grave,"
" Easy and slow on the jumper, will drive a hole for
    the blast,"
" Rome was long in the building, but the grandeur of
    Rome is past."

You speak of the road in your verses, you picture the
    joy of it still,
You of the specs and the collars, you who are geese of
    the quill,
You pad it along with a wine-flask and your pockets
    crammed with dough,
Eat and drink at your pleasure, and write how the
    flowers grow —
If your stomach was empty as pity, your hobnails were
    down at the heels,
And a nor'-easter biting your nose off, then you would
    know how it feels,
A nail in the sole of your bluchers jagging your foot
    like a pin,
And every step on your journey was driving it further
    in,

Then, out on the great long roadway, you'd find when
    you went abroad,
The nearer you go to nature the further you go from
    God.

Through many a sleepy hamlet, and many a noisy town,
While eyes of loathing stared us, we who were out and
    down,
Looking aslant at the wineshop, talking as lovers talk,
Of the lure of the gentle schooner, the joy of Carroll's
    Dundalk;
Sometimes bumming a pipeful, sometimes " shooting the
    crow," [1]
But ever onward and onward, fitfully, surely, slow,
On to the drill and the jumper, and on to the concrete
    bed,
On to the hovel and card school, the dirt-face, and
    slush ahead.

Thus was the long road followed — true is the tale I
    tell,
Ask my pals of the model — ask, they remember
    well —
Hear them tell how they tramped it, as they smoke at
    the bar and spit,
The journey to Ballachulish, for this is the song of it.

[1] Ordering drink, having no intention of paying for it.

SERFS

IN the lands that the leagueless and lonely, where
    fugitive, funeral-paced,
The day drags askance from the darkness to glower on
    the destitute waste,
Where raw-ribbed and desolate reaches ruggedly run
    to the sky,
Where the grim goring peaks of the mountains sunder
    the heavens on high,
Sullen and lowering and livid, furrowless, measureless,
    vast,
Pregnant with riches unravished, bearing a recordless
    past,
Hemmed with the mists of creation, ferine in fury for-
    lorn,
The wilderness reigneth malignant; and who may
    abide by its scorn,
Conquer the keeps of its splendour, looting the treasure
    it holds,
Damming its turbulent waters, rifling its forests and
    wolds,
Bridling its torrents with bridges, its mountain-cliffs
    battering down,
Turning its wastes to a garden, moulding its rocks to
    a town,
Flouting at famine and failure, sober to suffer and
    serve,
Staking their faith against danger in limitless daring
    and nerve,

Ne'er recking revenge nor repression, throttle the wild
    in its wrath,
Breaking the front of resistance unto the uttermost
    path?

And where shall you gather to dare it, men who are
    fearless and fit,
Primed with unquenchable courage, daring with Ber-
    serkir grit,
Freed from the cant of the city, purged of fastidious
    pride —
Men who will strive to a finish, men who are trusted
    and tried,
Emboldened by endless endeavour, steel-sinewed, bru-
    tish and wild —
Men with the tiger's insistence, and faith of an inno-
    cent child?
Go, seek them in pub and in model that steam with the
    stench of their shag,
Go, gather them up from the slumland and lure of the
    passionate hag,
Seek for the men of the highway, ragged, untutored
    and gaunt,
Men who can wrestle with horror and jeer at the ter-
    rors of want.
So one by one shall you gather them, one by one shall
    you send
Them over the pales of the city, where the roads that
    run outermost end.

And there in the primitive fastness, more like brutes
    than like men,
They're huddled in rat-riddled cabins, stuck in the
    feculent fen,

Where the red searing heat of the summer purges them
    drier than bone,
Where Medusa-faced winter in turn stiffens their
    limbs into stone.
Hemmed-up like fleas in the fissures, sweated like swine
    in the silt,
So that your deserts be conquered, so that your man-
    sions be built;
Hair-poised on the joist or the copestone, and swept by
    the bellowing gales,
Hauling their burdens of granite, bearing their mortar-
    piled pails,
Pacing the tremulous gang-planks as the trestles are
    bent by the wind,
With death and danger before them, and danger and
    death behind.
Where torments that terribly threaten engirdle the
    path that they tread,
As their bedfellows drop at the jumper, the brains
    blown out of the head,
Where misfires, burst in the boring, cripple the men as
    they fly,
And the dark-clotted blood on the hammer shall tell
    of the deaths that they die;
The eyes that are gouged from their sockets, the scars
    on the cankerous face
Of the hairy and horrible human, who drops at the
    quarry's base;
The wild arms tossed to the heavens, as the outworks
    crumble beneath,
The curse of surprise and of horror that is hissed
    through the closen teeth,
The derricks that break at their pivots with the strain
    of the burden they bear,
Crushing the men at the windlass before they can utter
    a prayer;

The dams rushing wild in the darkness, and hurtling
the flood-gates free,

The riotous rain-swollen rivers, that roll like an inland
sea

Swamping the mud-rimed cabins, and breaking them
up as they run,

Where men curse wild in the midnight, and die ere the
rising sun —

Die in the rush of the freshets screaming in fury and
fear,

As the timbers crunch in the torrent and jam in the
glutted weir;

There, gulping the chalice of sorrow and chewing the
crust of despair,

Thus do the slaves of the ages labour and dreadfully
dare,

Gripping the forelock of failure and bearing the brunt
of the fight,

For the crumbs that shall feed them at morning, the
bunks that shall rest them at night.

And there, stiff-lipped and enduring, stern-eyed, pa-
tient and rude,

Crushing the savage and sinister front of the lean
solitude,

Unto the ultimate barrier, unto the ultimate breath,

Lashed with the scourge of oppression, swept by the
legions of death,

They stumble like curs by the wayside, are flung in the
ditch where they die,

With never a stone to record them under the pitiless
sky;

Never a singer to chaunt them or tell of the deeds they
have done,

The passionate hates that pursued them, the battles
  they fought in and won —
How stark as the wilds where they labour, godlike they
  conquer or fall —
The courage, the dogged endeavour, the glory and woe
  of it all.

These are our serfs and our bondmen, slighted, for-
  saken, outcast,
Hewing the path of the future, heirs of the wrongs of
  the past,
Forespent in the vanguard of progress, vagrant, un-
  tutored, unskilled,
Labouring for ever and ever, so that our bellies be
  filled,
Building the homes of the haughty, rearing the man-
  sions of worth —
Wanderers lost to the wide world, hell-harried slaves
  of the earth,
Visionless, dreamless, and voiceless children of worry
  and care,
Sweltering, straining and striving under the burdens
  they bear —
Stretches the future before them clouded and bleak as
  their past
They are our serfs and our — brothers, slighted, for-
  saken, outcast.

D

LOVE

They sin who tell us love can die. — SOUTHEY.

LOVE will live while the pale stars glow, while the
world shall last,
On the present hopes, and in hours of woe, on a dreamy
past,
Love will live, while the flowers bloom, and the
meadows wave;
Nor yet be quenched by the charnel tomb — the
ghastly grave;
For o'er the tomb and the silver stars, to the gates
above
The soul will seek in the great Afar the Endless Love.

PLAYED OUT

AS a bullock falls in the crooked ruts, he fell when
the day was o'er,
The hunger gripping his stinted guts, his body shaken
and sore.
They pulled it out of the ditch in the dark, as a brute
is pulled from its lair,
The corpse of the navvy, stiff and stark, with the
clay on its face and hair.

In Christian lands, with calloused hands, he laboured
for others' good,
In workshop and mill, ditchway and drill, earnest,
eager and rude;
Unhappy and gaunt with worry and want, a food to
the whims of fate,
Hashing it out and booted about at the will of the
goodly and great.

To him was applied the scorpion lash, for him the gibe
and the goad —
The roughcast fool of our moral wash, the rugous
wretch of the road.
Willing to crawl for a pittance small to the swine of
the tinsel sty,
Beggared and burst from the very first, he chooses the
ditch to die —
. . . Go, pick the dead from the sloughy bed, and hide
him from mortal eye.

He tramped through the colourless winter land, or
　　swined in the scorching heat,
The dry skin hacked on his sapless hands or blistering
　　on his feet;
He wallowed in mire unseen, unknown, where your
　　houses of pleasure rise,
And hapless, hungry, and chilled to the bone, he builded
　　the edifice.

In cheerless model and filthy pub, his sinful hours were
　　passed,
Or footsore, weary, he begged his grub, in the sough
　　of the hail-whipped blast,
So some might riot in wealth and ease, with food and
　　wine be crammed,
He wrought like a mule, in muck to the knees, dirty,
　　dissolute, damned.

Arrogant, adipose, you sit in the homes he builded
　　high;
Dirty the ditch, in the depths of it he chooses a spot to
　　die,
Foaming with nicotine-tainted lips, holding his aching
　　breast,
Dropping down like a cow that slips, smitten with
　　rinderpest;
Drivelling yet of the work and wet, swearing as sinners
　　swear,
Raving the rule of the gambling school, mixing it up
　　with a prayer.

He lived like a brute, as the navvies live, and went as
　　the cattle go,

No one to sorrow and no one to shrive, for heaven or-
dained it so —
He handed his check to the shadow in black, and went
to the misty lands,
Never a mortal to close his eyes or a woman to cross
his hands.

As a bullock falls in the rugged ruts
   He fell when the day was o'er.
Hunger gripping his weasened guts,
   But never to hunger more —
They pulled it out of the ditch in the dark,
   The chilling frost on its hair,
The mole-skinned navvy stiff and stark
   From no particular where.

THE WOE OF IT

SWEET was the mavis' song of eld,
  And how the woodlands thrilled with it!
Sweeter the song of the girl I held
  Close to the heart that filled with it.

Methinks the rose leant from the wall
  To kiss the lily brow of hers;
And through the years I can recall
  The softly whispered vow of hers.

We saw the evening fade afar,
  And parting, never met again;
And ere we meet, how many a star
  Shall rise again and set again.

The mavis' song but brings regret,
  The fading rose must know of it:
For she is gone — I can't forget,
  And — ah! the bitter woe of it!

THE LONG ROAD

THE white road leads through the meadows, on
    through the sunshine and shadows,
  The endless road to anywhere, the road the navvy
    knows;
Where the mountains soar in their starkness, piercing
    the light and the darkness,
  The thin road lies like a ribbon, he follows it where
    it goes.

He has seen the dewdrops cluster where modest daisies
    muster,
  He has lain on earth's soft bosom, watched by the
    Milky Way,
Out in the places lonely, with the stars and the silence
    only,
  Chilled with the hate of Winter, warmed with the
    love of May.

He has padded alone, while the vagrant breezes bore
    him the fragrant
  Scent of the wayside flowers, or blooms from the
    hills afar,
He has listened the torrents grumble at the hills from
    which they tumble,
  He has seen the soft night kneeling to greet the even-
    ing star.

  .   .   .   .

Tired of the reeking hovel, weary of pick and shovel,
  He wanders out on the white road in the evening's
    sheen of gold,

Watching the light that dims on the western hills of
  crimson,
  And longs for the last lone slumber and knows he is
  growing old.

He goes from the ones who knew him, those who were
  kindly to him,
  Out on the lonely roadway, under the starlit dome,
And follows the path that flies on into the dim horizon
  Where the spectral moon-fire lies on the road that
  leads to home.

HAVE YOU —

(On the road to Kinlochleven, 1908.)

HAVE you tramped about in Winter, when your
  boots were minus soles?
Have you wandered sick and sorry with your pockets
  full of — holes?
Have you wondered which was better, when your capi-
  tal was light,
A plate of fish and taters, or a hammock for the night?
Have you smelt the dainty odour of some swell re-
  freshment shop,
When you 'd give your soul in barter for a single
  mouldy chop?
Have you sought through half the kingdom for the job
  you could not get?
Have you eyed the city gutters for a stump of
  cigarette?
Have you dossed in drear December on a couch of
  virgin snow
With a quilt of frost above you and a sheet of ice
  below?

These are incidental worries which are wrong to fuss
  about;
But God! they matter greatly to the man who 's down
  and out.

Have you sweltered through the Summer, till the salt
  sweat seared your eyes?
Have you dragged through plumb-dead levels in the
  slush that reached your thighs?
Have you worked the weighty hammer swinging heavy
  from the hips,

While the ganger timed the striking with a curse upon
his lips?
Have you climbed the risky gang-plank where a bird
might fear to stop,
And reckoned twenty fathoms would be hellish far to
drop?
Have you swept the clotted point-rods and the red-
dened reeking cars
That have dragged a trusty comrade through the
twisted signal bars?
Have you seen the hooded signal, as it swung above
you clear,
And the deadly engine rushing on the mate who
did n't hear?

If you want to prove your manhood in the way the
navvies do,
These are just the little trifles that are daily up to you.
And if you have n't shared the risk, the worry and
the strife,
Disappointment, and the sorrow, then you know not
what is life.

Have you padded through the country when the Sum-
mer land was fair,
And the white road lay before you leading on just any-
where?
Have you seen the dusk grow mellow, and the break-
ing morn grow red,
And the little diamond dew-drops come to sentinel
your bed?
Though your clothes were rather shabby, and your toes
and knees were bare,
The little silly birdies sure they did n't seem to care;

But just sang to cheer your journey, as they would to
cheer a prince,
For they saw old Adam naked, and they know no
better since.

Have you slouched along the meadows, have you smelt
the new-mown hay?
Have you smoked your pipe and loved it as you plodded
on the way?
Have you bummed your bit of tucker from the matron
at the door
And blessed the kindly woman who had pity on the
poor?
A pipe of strong tobacco (if you get it) after meals
And there's many a scrap of comfort for the man
who's down at heels.

Have you felt your blood go rushing, and your heart
beat strangely high,
As the smoke of your tobacco curled upwards to the
sky,
When lying 'neath a spreading tree that shaded from
the sun
The happiest mortal in the land, it dared not shine
upon.
If you have n't shared the pleasure, that follows after
strife,
You do not know the happiness that fills a navvy's life.

THE SONG OF THE DRAINER

(On Toward Mountain, 1907.)

HE is the Drainer. —
   Out on the moorland bleak and grey, using his
spade in a primitive way, through chilly evening and
searing day.   Call him a fool, and well you may —
                              He is the Drainer.

The toil of the Drainer. —
   Only the simple work to do, to plod and delve the
quagmire through, for thirty pence, his daily screw. —
The labour is healthy — but not for you,
                              Just for the Drainer.

The artless Drainer. —
   It does n't require a lot of skill to dig with a spade
or hammer a drill, but it 's bad enough for a man when
ill with fevery bones or a wintry chill —
                              Even a Drainer.

The home of the Drainer. —
   A couple of stakes shoved into the ground, a hole for
a window, a roof tree crowned with rushes and straw,
and all around a waste where lichens and weeds abound.
                              Is the home of the Drainer.

The rugged Drainer. —
   The sleepy bog breezes chant their hymn, the rushes
and lilies are soft and slim, the deep dark pools the sun-
beams limn — but what do these beauties matter to
him —
                              The rugged Drainer?

The poor old Drainer. —

Some day he 'll pass away in a cramp, where the sundews gleam and the bogbines ramp, and go like a ghost from the drag and the damp — the poor old slave of the dismal swamp.

The hapless Drainer.

Such is the Drainer. —

Voiceless slave of the solitude, rude as the draining shovel is rude — Man by the ages of wrong subdued, marred, misshapen, misunderstood —

Such is the Drainer.

THE BALLAD OF MACINDOE

MACINDOE was a Scotchman — had other fail-
ings, too,
Unco sour and moody, hankered as Scotchmen do
After the gill almighty — bibulous MacIndoe!

Out on a steamer southward breasting a heavy swell,
The captain roared, " To the lifeboats," MacIndoe
roared " To H——,"
And stood by a whiskey barrel aboard of the Heather
Bell.

Out in the teeth of the swirling, ranting, riotous sea,
The yardarms battered to larboard, the hatchways
shattered to lee —
(Something like that he told me — the cook of the
Buzzy Bee.)

The Bell went this way and that way, forward and
back again,
Then sank on the seething billows, leaving poor Mac
alane,
Perched on a whiskey barrel out on the Spanish main.

But his was a courage undaunted, courage that never
could fail,
He placed himself up for a mainmast, spread out his
coat for a sail,
And wondering where he was going, he drifted before
the gale.

On to his slippery foothold grimly and gaunt he clung,
Till daybreak its shafts of carmine over the waters
   flung —
" Noo," said the thirsty sailor, " I think I 'll tak' oot
   the bung."

But the plans o' a moose or sailor gang aften times
   agley,
And you 'll hardly open a barrel, labour and tug as
   you may,
Out on the frivolous ocean in the old methodical way.

So Sandy found to his terror, and cursed his luckless
   star,
That poor benighted, sweating, swearing, sorrowing
   tar,
Who murmured loud in his anguish, " So near and yet
   so far."

He watched the languid ocean in leisurely wavelets
   roll ;
The fiery sun in the heaven was scorching his very
   soul —
" Oh, for a raft of an iceberg, near tae the Arctic
   Pole."

He seated himself on his barrel and pondered on Auld
   Lang Syne,
Brose and bannocks and Burns, water and women and
   wine,
Then scooped up the waves of the ocean, and drank of
   the arid brine.

Below the sensuous waters, above him the heavens
   grim —

What was it rose for a moment ominous, vague and
    dim?
MacIndoe shuddered in horror — a shark was follow-
    ing him!

Night came dreary and darkling, he saw the cleaving
    fin
Of the fish draw near and nearer, ugly and fell as
    sin —
" God," said the shivering sailor, " such a fix to be in! "

He tore his coat to ribbons and lashed himself to his
    raft,
Slept, and dreamt of devils, woke from his sleep and
    laughed,
There was the sign of the monster slowly following aft.

The moon was up in the heavens ghastly, gibbous and
    wan,
But not as pale as the lonely, sorrowful, sinful mon,
Who, tied to a whiskey barrel, waited till day would
    dawn.

Day and the young day's blushes spread away to the
    rear,
The man stood up on his timbers and feared with a
    deadly fear,
There was the fin of the monster ever approaching near.

Opal and ruby and diamond glimmered the eastern
    sky,
And the waters that circled the barrel laughed to the
    sun on high,
" Christ! " — and the sailor shuddered, " a beautiful
    day to die."

He thought of the mother who bore him, he thought
of the homely croft,
Where the heath of the hill was purple, the grass of
the field was soft,
Then he looked to the sky above him, and thought of
the God aloft.

He ventured to kneel to heaven and pray for a drop of
rain,
His knees were creaking and aching, he moaned as a
child in pain,
But found he forgot what the words were, and rose to
his feet again.

Down in the deep below him he saw the sword fish
swim,
The weird uncanny spectres rise from their caverns
dim,
But one still stayed on the surface waiting he knew for
him.

Morning and night and morning, light and darkness
and light,
Hungry when stars were beaming, thirsty when noon
was bright,
Hungry and tired and thirsty and — Heavens, a sail
in sight!

They picked him up from the ocean, the grinning, gib-
bering Gael,
Nude as a nymph on his barrel, using his shirt for a
sail —
Thus they told it to me on the Buzzy Bee,
But I never believed the tale.

E

THE SONG OF MALONEY

THEY are gambling in the cabin, Moleskin Joe,
   Magee and Dan,
   There's a splash of stagnant crimson on the lance-
      edged hills afar —
I've a whiff of good tobacco, and a bucket in the can,
   And a sort of fawning liking for the trembling
      evening star,
And my thoughts go roaming, roaming, like an exile's
   in the gloaming,
   Through the grey fogs of the valley and the cloud
      wreaths of the hill,
And I think I see her yet, where in olden days we met,
   Awaiting at the corner for her bloke returning still.

Moleskin's plunging bob and tanner, he would call me
   such a fool
   If he knew what I was thinking in the heel-end of
      the day,
But somehow I cannot help it, and I cannot bear the
   school,
   For my thoughts are ever running to a maiden miles
      away,
To a maiden hellish pretty, in the dirty, smoky
   city,
   Poor as me she is, and poorer, but a year or two
      ago,
Ere I came to swine in muck where all nature's down
   on luck,
   She was more to me I reckon than anyone I know.

O'er the dam, across the breastworks, drops the night
and fills the land,
    There are lights inside the cabin, there are many at
the game,
But away down in the city does she ever under-
stand
    The reason that I 'm lagging, and the why I never
came? —
Maybe she 's forgot about me, plodding on her own
without me,
    I the roughest card among us, I the plunger at the
school,
And the pallid evening star whispers, " Idiot that you
are!
    Do you really think she wants you, you a whiskey-
sodden fool? "

Down behind the mountain ridges, grave-like valleys
gulp the night,
    Far below the grave-like valleys lies the town of
which I dream,
With its many lamps aglitter, and the music halls
alight,
    And the galleries are crowded, and the footlights
are agleam,
And perhaps the actress singing, some fond memories is
bringing
    Of the kisses in the alley, and the softly whispered
vow —
Here I 'm dreaming miles away, she is sitting at the
play,
    Maybe thinking kindly of me as I 'm thinking of her
now.

And the photo that she gave me, on the lonely night
we parted

I have lost it, 't was the night we tried to clear the
McSurly's bar —

" Come, Maloney, fill the school up — " Well, when-
ever you have started

On the downward road, its smoother than the other
road by far —

All right, Carroty, I 'm willing, I have got an extra
shilling —

Mary Somers, oh, she 's hooked up by some collared
city chap,

But perhaps I 'll meet her yet, for somehow I can't
forget —

Shut up, Moleskin, here I 'm coming, is it banker,
brag, or nap?

BAD NEWS

(McSurly's Bar.)

He hugged a delusion in petticoats. — MOLESKIN.

" YOUR flame is marri'd I understand,"
   He heard the man from the city say,
He dealt the flats with a shaky hand [1]
   And clean forgot the manner of play;
I saw his eyelids quiver a bit,
   And Big Maloney was never a saint,
He played the game, made a mess of it,
   Yet his partner saw it without complaint.

He shoved the fingers to beat the four,
   And led the queen for another's ace,
Then jacked his hand and staked no more,
   So Carroty Dan took up his place.
He sat apart on the wooden seat
   Pulling a clay that was not alight,
Shaking his head, and shuffling his feet —
   Maloney was out of sorts that night.

I noticed the lines on his haggard face,
   I heard him sigh. We played the game —
" Moleskin, lead." He led the ace;
   Carroty Dan had the Jack for the same.
Some muttered: " There 's more fish in the sea,"
   And others remarked: " A maid 's a maid,"
" There is n't another girl for me,"
   Was all that Big Maloney said.

[1] He becometh poor who dealeth with a slack hand. —
Prov. x., 4.

Poor Maloney! And still we played —
   "Where, M'Kay, is the trump you gave?"
"Well, it is queer," another said,
   "I thought he'd play on his mother's grave."
But Jim Maloney was looking sad,
   Another fellow had hooked his flame,
And some remarked, "Is it not too bad?"
   As we shuffled the cards and played the game.

THE PASSING OF MALONEY

IN the chill of anæmic December when the snow on
the ditchway lay,
He bursted the jaw of the gaffer, in an argumentative
way [1]
Got handed his couple of shillings and went in the
evening grey —

Into the dip of the hollow a moving speck on the snow,
Bound for the township and model, eighty miles off
or so,
And his comrades leaned on their shovels, and sorrowed
to see him go.

That night they kept from the card school, and smoked
in silence apart,
Swore at the cloud-drift, and listened the night winds
fitfully start,
And felt a chill in the marrow or an icy grip on the
heart.

Quickly he padded the mountain, and dragged thro'
the desolate vale,
And over the gap-toothed ridges, where the flaccid sun-
sets fail,
And the endless cumulus musters glaucous or flaxen
pale.

[1] The opinion of the man who argues with his fist is always
respected. — From the Diary of Moleskin Joe.

Broad-chested, lank Maloney, muscular, strong and
    wild,
A Berserkir fierce in his anger, simple in faith as a
    child,
The primitive human in moleskin, uncultured and
    undefiled.

Crunching and crushing the snow-way, cursing his
    luck when he fell,
He plodded unweary, unfearing, by quagmire and tarn
    and well,
And a star o'erhead where the cloudrift spread gleamed
    like an asphodel,

Gleamed for a tremulous moment, fading as soon as
    it shone,
Leaving him lost in the vastness of night and its by-
    ways unknown,
With a charnel gloominess girded, affrighted, astray
    and alone.

Otiose, obdurate, ominous, drifted the snow in the air,
Gibingly, grim, geomantic, tracing the lines of despair,
Weaving a shroud for his body, shaping a wreath for
    his hair.

" Where am I straying to anyhow? Cold! I am cold
    to the skin. . . .
Lord, he's a hell of a gaffer! . . how did the quarrel
    begin?
Called me an imp of the devil, and managed to get me
    my tin.

" I 'm sure I am lost in the darkness — ain't it a hor-
rible fix,
Knowing your final is coming. . . . Curse him, the
imp of old Nick's.
Every foot that I 'm lifting drags like a bundle of
bricks.

" I 'm padding it round in a circle — round in a circle
— and round. . . .
To-morrow they 'll search and they 'll find me, dead
like a brute on the ground.
Dead! . . 'T is the corpse of Maloney, Moleskin will
say when I 'm found.

" Mary, the girl that I courted — how under hell can
it be —
There she 's smiling . . . she 's calling, calling and
beckoning me!
Look at the swarm of demons — and grinning like
blazes they be.

" Shoving it on to a fellow, 'cause you are boss of the
show. . . .
Here I am raving and raving, wandering round in the
snow,
Going to hell in a blizzard — well, it is time I should
go!

" Drinks to the bar and I 'll stand it, everyone here in
the place. . . .
Turn a man off in the snow-drift — go, or I 'll batter
your face. . . .
Matey, my turn at the hammer — I 'm for a bob on
the ace."

He jacked up his soul in the darkness, and slept in an
    angel white shroud,
And the ghouls of the moorland kept litchwake under
    the canopied cloud,
When nature was yelling in anguish and the turbulent
    tempest was loud.

THE GRAVE DIGGER

I spoke to a man once; asking what he thought of going back
to the land and having small holdings. "Very good," he said,
"in fact the solution of all ills."
Afterwards I learned that he was a grave-digger.
— From "Gleanings from a Navvy's Scrap-Book."

If some people rose from the dead and read their epitaphs they
would think they had got into the wrong graves!
— MOLESKIN JOE.

A GRIM old man with a weazened visage —
What does he dream of toiling there?
Rest should be meet for a man of his age,
Old and weary — but who may care?
There, when the dawn's bright pennon waves,
There, when the fleeting eve fails dimly,
Aloof and alone he labours grimly,
Earning a living, digging graves.

So much a grave, and a soul's in Heaven:
So much a grave, and a soul's in Hell:
For old-world death makes matters even,
The sexton profits, and all is well.
All is well — but the lover raves,
And tears are wet on the downcast lashes.
"Dust to dust, and ashes to ashes,"
Ponders the sexton, digging graves.

Some go into the House of Pleasure,
Some go into the House of Gloom;
The miser hoards up his garnered treasure,
The treasure the rust and moth consume.

Alas! for the wealth the miser saves,
In the House of Pain or the House of Passion.
" He 'll need it not in the House I fashion " —
Chuckles the sexton, digging graves.

All are his tenants, lord and lady,
Villain and harlot of low degree,
Simpering saint, and sinner shady,
Every manner of companie,
Their homes with brainless skulls he paves,
Lily white as alabaster.
" Even the brainless know I 'm master,"
Muses the sexton, digging graves.

But there he labours, the cynic sexton,
For all men toil and the sexton must;
Waiting betimes for the silent next one,
Next — not last, to the House of dust.
This is the Home of squires and slaves,
Still from the hall, and stiff from the hovel.
" I 'll house them alike with my pick and shovel,"
Chuckles the sexton, digging graves.

A SPRING IDYLL

ON my hangings of arras
  Dewdrop and sunlight commingle,
The music of woods that are endless,
And infinite seas
    That come with the voices
    Of storm or of calm to the shingle
In the lilac grey blush of the dawn,
On the sensuous breeze.

So full of promise is earth
  As a child's gentle laughter,
  The sapphire tints of the water
  Are fair to the eyes —
    The present is only,
    I know not a past nor hereafter,
  And forth from my covering
  Of saffron and ermine I rise.

MY DREAM GIRL

L IKE a flower in the mist of the moorland, spectral,
        shadowy,
Is she the girl of my dreamings, simple and fawn-like
        shy;
Hers the ethereal radiance of heavenly groves and
        streams;
Such as the painter pictures, such as the poet dreams.

Out in the open spaces she beckons my spirit on,
She that is born of evening, and fades in the lilac dawn.
She comes from the ports of the flaxen moon on one of
        the spirit ships,
Her tresses are night's abysses, the red rose gleams on
        her lips,
Through the soft, impalpable ether she has ordered her
        ship to go,
By Peristan of the musk-winds, where snow-white spice
        flowers blow;
On the manes of the crooning breezes, by fairy lands
        untold,
She comes in the guise of a mortal, who never groweth
        old;
Through the tangle of gossamer silver the bow of her
        vessel cleaves,
And the moonlight opens before it with a rustle of
        willow leaves,
Down to the fringe of the moorland where the land
        and the heavens meet,
Where the quivering bloom of the heather presses to
        kiss her feet,

Prankt in a robe of star-mist tinged with its many
    dyes.
And I watch as a lover watches till the transient vision
    flies —
The mystic girl of my dreamings, simple and fawn-like
    shy,
The flower in the mist of the moorland, lonesome and
    shadowy.

LOGIC

" PALMAM qui meruit ferat " — he who wins the
    palm should bear it, for I certainly admit,
Being but the super-navvy, burdened with the hod,
    vous-savez, I 've no wish to carry it.
I don't pose as one who knows an awful lot about
    Spinoza, or some other ancient seer,
I don't wear a sort of faintly dawning, growing, super-
    saintly imitation of a sneer,
But withal I 've a prolific knowledge of the scientific
    which I 've picked up here and there,
And a little super-added from the lore of those who
    pad it on the road to anywhere.

In my knockabout existence, on the line of least re-
    sistance, I have plodded day by day,
And of course from the beginning I have done a lot of
    sinning in a very vulgar way,
And you 'll find I 'm no exception in æsthetical percep-
    tion of the art that lies in lies,
So each item of my tale is to be read, cum grano salis,
    as it will, since ye are wise.

Here a man lays money by him.   My life's rule is
    " Carpe diem," and at last a day will be
When they 'll gladly write, " Hic Jacet," on a marble
    slab and place it over him; but as for me,
Everyone can do without me, no one cares a damn
    about me, no one 's sorry when I slide —
But it is a trifle funny, when he 's dead, the man of
    money, someone 's hellish satisfied.

I am one of those who know it, it takes more to make
 a poet than a mass of flowing hair,
I have tried the thing already, so my friend, " Experto
 crede," listen to me and beware.
Homer was a parish beggar, Burns had to measure
 lager, or some other beverage,
Poor old Villon had to take a jemmy in his hand to
 make an ill-begotten living wage —
What 's the good of writing of the stars and skies that
 are above the world you rhyme upon so well —
Rhyme in sentimental gushes of your Angelina's blushes
 — if your verses do not sell?

. . . .

I have read Montaigne and Dante in the dead end or
 the shanty, which you 'll certainly agree
May be due in greatest measure to the economic pres-
 sure and the hurried times that be —
" Otium cum dignitate," for some problem rather
 weighty, certainly I 've never had,
For you 'll find it hard to learn, all the views of Kant
 or Sterne, hashing on the barrow squad —
But apart from that the fact is, if you put it into prac-
 tice, put your knowledge into rhyme,
Do it up as this is done up, spin it up as this is spun
 up, you are scoring every time.

. . . .

There are lots of folks who clamour that the man who
 strikes the hammer, cannot, though he likes to, rise
From the squalor of the masses to the glory of Par-
 nassus, which I might remark is lies —
'Tis a pretty wide expansion from the muckpile to the
 mansion, some, and many still may rave,
Yet they know (at least they ought to) that tho' far
 removed it 's not too far from either to the grave.

F

I have taken oft the oddest little moment for a modest
　　glance at Tolstoy or at Taine,
While the boss was kicking hell up I 've been trying to
　　develop the resources of my brain,
Or when burst as burst at nap I meditated quite un-
　　happy on the lore of ancient fools,
On some grim platonic sages who had never lost their
　　wages in the fishy gambling schools,
On the white road leading through the land of " No one
　　wants you," to the land of " What you should
　　have done,"
I have plodded day and daily, sometimes woeful, some-
　　times gaily, brother of the wind and sun,

For companions I have taken — Shakespeare, Old
　　Khayyam, or Bacon and have sat beneath the
　　bough,
But no loaf and flask was near me, so old Bacon
　　could n't cheer me — Shakespeare had forgotten
　　how —
Though a lack of education makes one lack appreciation
　　of the greatest minds of earth,
Still you 'll find that ne'er a rub is harder borne than
　　lack of grub is, while you estimate their worth.

　·　　·　　·　　·　　·　　·　　·　　·　　·

If a man says, " Gee up, Neddy," in uncultured word
　　and ready, suffer him and let him pass,
" Proceed, Edward " is so toffish that it seems a little
　　offish, when you say it to an ass —
So I hope my wisdom scraps will be esteemed — but
　　they perhaps will be regarded just as lies,
And remember that my tale is to be read, " cum grano
　　salis," as it will, for you are wise.

BOREAS

HE threw the pine tree in the fiord,
  And down the spumous seas he hurled
The jagged iceberg of the north
  To languish in a stagnant world,
And o'er the highway of the skies
  The clouds impetuously whirled.

Upon the bald, blank hill we met,
  He blustered in insensate wrath,
He caught and flung me like a child,
  He shook and bent me like a lath,
Because I dared to flaunt his power,
  Because I ventured on his path.

" Zephyrus, Eurus, Africus,
  Boreas, Auster, Aquilo,
Or one or all, I know not which,
  And care not though I do not know,
Why use your means to work me harm?
  And bash and birl and bend me so?

" The flashing lightnings pierce you through,
  You bluster vainly at the hill,
Ten thousand times you beat his crest,
  Ten million, and he flaunts you still;
You are the fettered slave of man,
  You bow obedient to his will."

" You — you — unblushingly you rave
　Of all the pigmy deeds of men —
I 've swept across the clay that was
　Or Paladin or Saracen,
When naked Adam blushed for shame
　I gloried in my starkness then!

" I saw the might of Babylon,
　I saw the verdant fields of Thrace,
I marked the Romans in their power,
　I 've seen them in their dire disgrace —
I am; they were, and Cæsar now
　Can't wipe the maggot off his face.

" Where is the glory that was Greece?
　Let Athens' crumbling walls reply —
Where is the pride of Nineveh,
　Thou shivering fool of destiny?
Between the earth and sky I 've borne
　The ashes that were Pompeii!

" What is the pride you rave of worth?
　What are the things that you have done?
Are all your deeds of deathless fame
　From David to Napoleon,
A musty coffin full of dust,
　A grimly grinning skeleton?

" I bear the scent of briar and rose
　Through all the lover-ionged-for June,
I hurl the death-black clouds athwart
　The silvern oceans of the moon,
I am Siroc and Harmattan,
　Solano, Mistral, and Simoon.

" Upon the proud Armada I
   Came vengeful and in dreadful shape,
I drove its ships through goaded seas
   Where slimy-walled the fissures gape
In many a gloomy, deadly bluff,
   In many a chasmed, tusk-edged cape.

" The ringed and sworded buccaneers,
   They blessed me in the siren breeze,
I lured the Vikings wild and rude
   Across the icy northern seas,
And then I laughed their faith to scorn,
   And swept their laden argosies.

" Beyond the reaches of the stars,
   Impearled byways of the night,
In dark abyssmal zarahs, far
   I 've ventured on my endless flight,
Beyond the thrones of gods unknown,
   And margents of the infinite."

He came I wist not whence, nor where,
   The bluster ready on his lip,
He fled, and left me wondering,
   Impotent, helpless, from his grip —
Despite it all, I felt with him
   A sort of roving fellowship.

THE NAVVY CHORUS [1]

'TWAS in the beginning of ages,
  To the make of the navvy there came
Work and the lowest of wages
  Ever a mortal could claim,
Bread, with its age for leaven,
  Rows, and the prison cell,
Few of the gifts of heaven,
  And most of the vices of hell,
Time, and dislike to do it,
  Love, for the wine when red,
And a bibulous leaning to it
  Despite what the sages said.

And the demons took in hand
  Moleskin, leather, and clay,
Oaths embryonic and
  A longing for Saturday,
Kneestraps and blood and flesh,
  A chest exceedingly stout,
A soul — (which is a ques-
  tion open to many a doubt),
And fashioned with pick and shovel,
  And shapened in mire and mud,
With life of the road and hovel,
  And death of the line or hod,
With fury and frenzy and fear
  That his strength might endure for a span
From birth, through beer to bier,
  The link 'twixt the ape and the man.

[1] *Cp.* Swinburne. *Atalanta in Calydon*, Shepherd's Chorus.

They gave him a will to strive
  And earn the pittance which
Can barely keep him alive
  To slave in the dirty ditch —
Poorhouse and prison they wrought,
  So he might enter therein
When idleness fell his lot
  Or poverty led to sin.
They have given him transient joys,
  They have given him space for delight,
The model, its riot and noise,
  And night, and the fleas of the night,
The jeer of the better dressed neighbour,
  And curses to every breath,
Labour, and dodging of labour,
  Foreknowledge of sudden death —
Foredoomed to go to the devil,
  He carries a swearing gift.[1]
His life is a path of evil
  Between a shift and a shift.

[1] Swearing is not a habit but a gift. — From the Diary of Moleskin Joe.

TWENTY–ONE

We spend our years as a tale that is told badly. — From Moleskin Joe's Diary.

DOSSING it here in the model, dreary, bedraggled, dry,
They're cooking their grub on the hot-plate, and I have got none to fry,
But still there's a bed for twopence, so I'll go to sleep if I can,
Go a boy to my slumber and rise to-morrow a man.

Twenty and one to-morrow, twenty and one and not
A cent for the weary years that with shovel and bar I've wrought —
Out on my own since childhood, down on my luck since birth,
I who belong to the holiest civilized land on earth.

I've done my graft on the dead line, where the man with the muck-rake is,
Where the model smells I have dossed it in this woeful world of His,
While others were spending their springtime learning to please and pray,
I've fought for my right of living my own particular way.

Oft I put cash to the bankers, banked it and lost till broke,
Watching it tanner by tanner pass to the sharper's poke,

And many a night in the hovel brag was the game we
  played,
When I who was versed in the shovel fell to a heavy
  spade.

Horses ran on the race course and won as a matter of
  course —
I 've lost a tribe of money backing the other horse.
Beer, the hope of the dead-line! beer, the joy of the
  soul!
Why would I pine and worry when beer can make me
  whole? [1]

And money is round to go round.   Horses and wine,
  and yes,
Women are fond of finery, women are fond of dress —
Oh, pretty as girls are pretty, usual hair and eyes,
Golden and blue, etcetera, choke full of smiles and sighs.

Eyes of a luring siren, a hell of a blarneying tongue,
Old are the arts of women, and I was so very young,
Another came round to woo her, and sudden she took
  to it,
I hugged a delusion in hairpins, got done like a frog
  on the spit.

Seven years on the muck-pile — God, but I 'm feeling
  sick!
Sick of the slush and the shovel, sick of the hammer
  and pick,
Labour endless and thankless, labour that 's never
  done —
Is it sinful to doubt of Heaven at penniless twenty-one?

[1] Let him drink and forget his poverty. — Prov. xxxi., 7.

Not the price of a schooner, and, Lord, but I 'm feeling
 dry;
They 're grubbing it up on the hot-plate, but I 've got
 nothing to fry —
Still I can doss on twopence, and I 'll go to sleep if
 I can —
Go a boy to my slumber and rise to-morrow a man!

THE WATERS

PLACID it lies as death and passionless as the grave,
  With the pallid moonbeams flung like corpse-lights
    o'er its wave,
Stuck in the hunch-backed hill, sluggish, silent, apart,
Brooding in durance vile, sad in its inmost heart,
Whimpering around the face, the sluice and the hard-
    fast wall,
The great dam slumbers alone, sore of its endless
    thrall —
Down at the slimy base men toil in the dreary pit,
Under the shadow of night, cowering under it.

Freed from their prison walls, glad from the pent-up
    place,
Down the trough of the hill streamlets on streamlets
    race
Mad with the joy they feel, full of a wild desire,
Springing from ledge to ledge in molten silvery fire.

One by one they rise, the makeshift, rough-cast huts,
Where the knoll across the run of the little waters juts,
Here by the hot-plate's glow the shivering, shabby
    tramp
Spells out the " Betting News " in the glare of the
    naphtha lamp,
One man handles his gold, another writes to his love,
In the reeking gloomy hut in the shade of the dam
    above,

A dozen crowd to the school, watching the gamblers
    play —

*   *   *

A crash on the face of the hill, and the maddened dam
    gives way!

A swirl, and the walls go down, the walls and the
    watchers both,
A screech as the girders jamb — a prayer that is half
    an oath;
The sluggish sand-hole spews, swallows and spews again,
The cesspool fills and chokes the throat of the sated
    drain.

The flood breaks over the wall, foaming in ecstasy,
The black mud scurries before as it shivers the sluices
    free,
The mountain shrubs uptorn, effortless share its path,
It madly whirls on the bend in all its riotous wrath.

"Winning! a running flush — *Christ! has the dam
    gone loose!*"
The tramp gets up with a curse, grasping his
    "Betting News,"
The gamblers gather their stakes, curious, undismayed,
The miser grabs at his wealth, the lover rises afraid,
The bulging wall breaks in, the roof falls through at
    a blow,
A moment to think of a prayer, and breathe it before
    they go —
A moment, and then the flood reels through the broken
    wall,
Caught like fleas in the fire, they splutter and choke
    and fall —

Down the face of the hill, the waters roar as they
    spread,
Bearing in braggart glee their freight of unshriven dead.

*They builded a wall of stone with cunning, patience and
    skill,*
And the waters sulked behind brooding on every ill,
*Till their pent-up rage broke forth on the men who
    curbed their will.*

THE BALLAD OF THE LONG DAM

'TWAS on the day the Dam gave way, I mind it
    awfully well,
Moleskin Joe and Carroty Dan had a row about Riley's
    gel —
Good for a chew! Well, seeing it 's you, I think I 'll
    yarn it out;
Just turn your eye on that wall hard by, and see is the
    boss about.

Wal, first let me tell how Riley's gel was pretty as
    women go,
And whiles she went out with Carroty Dan, and whiles
    she went out with Joe,
The way of a man with a maid, 't is said, is strange,
    and it 's scripture true,
But stranger by far you 'll find they are, the wonder-
    ful ways of two.

Day in and out it was fight about, night after night
    the same,
And they batter it here, a trifle queer, as there ain't
    no rules in the game,
A throw or a grip, a kick or a trip, no wool-padded,
    kid-gloved play
You can go for your man in any style your own pe-
    culiar way.

'T was on the day the Long Dam burst, Moleskin he
    bummed his sub,

And went and got boozed as he often did down at the
    nearest pub,
Primed to the neck he weltered back, and sought out
    Carroty D.,
And the rest of us quickly formed a ring for the fight
    that we knew would be.

'T was a fight and a half that blessed day, and as hard
    as ever I saw,
Moleskin Joe had the track of a blow of a shoe on his
    bearded jaw,
Carroty Dan had some teeth bunged out, and his eyes
    bunged up as well,
When some one shouted, " The Long Dam 's burst,
    slide like the very hell ! "

We heard the piles in the breastwork creek, break like
    a twig and fall,
We saw the riotous water crash over the broken wall,
The roots and the furze and the rocks uphurled, go
    like a wash of snow,
Then sudden I minded of Riley's gel alone in the hut
    below —

Alone in the path of the loosened flood. . . . I ran
    like the very wind,
With hurl and groan, by hollow and stone, I heard it
    breaking behind,
I heard it urge its curling surge to the moan of the
    failing stay,
And charge the banks in endless ranks forcing its head-
    strong way.

And still the waters vomited forth, on cabin and copse
    and bent,

And still on my errand lightning-winged over the ridge
　　　I went —
How I got saved, and how we were saved, is more than
　　　I 'm fit to tell,
But I mind of beating it by a neck along with old
　　　Riley's gel.

That is the tale.　'T is a dirty job, and ours is a rotten
　　　trade,
It takes a while to gather a pile with the help of a
　　　shovel and spade —
There 's Moleskin there a-shovelling dirt, and Car-
　　　roty with a hod,
And Riley's daughter 's married to me — honest, so help
　　　me God.

" HELL! "

(McSurly's Bar, 1911.)

COME gather, boys, together and we 'll gulp a cup
  to cheer us,
  Tho' the night is slinking past, let us be blythe,
We have done our graft and stuck it, boys, though
  death was ever near us
  All the way from Kinlochleven to Rosyth.
We have wrought in all the wide world's outside
  reaches,
  And you 'll never find us chickens at our work;
We have clinched with toil and terror, and have mated
  woe and error —
  'T was up to us, and, boys, we did n't shirk.

But 't was hell — pure hell — the while it lasted,
  And cursèd little wages for the pain,
But 't was up to us to do it, and by Cripes we managed
  thro' it,
  And to-morrow —it will be the same again.

Do you mind the nights we laboured, boys, together,
  Spread-eagled at our travail on the joists;
With the pulley wheels a-turning and the naphtha
  lamps a-burning,
  And the mortar crawling upward on the hoists,
While our hammers clanked like blazes on the facing
  Where the trestles shook and staggered as we struck,
While the derricks on their pivots strained and broke
  the crank-wheel rivets
  As the shattered jib sank heavy in the muck.

  G

It was hell — pure hell — from start to finish,
  And when it 's done, our labour will atone,
For all we did in strife and wrong the wild and erring
    life along —
  Of us, who know the hell of it alone.

Do you mind the nights we fought, and drank and
    lusted
  When the wild red blood was up and sense was
    gone,
There is much we can discuss about, and plenty too to
    curse about,
  The brutal lusts that led forever on.
How we wooed the bright-eyed women of the gutter,
  How we squared our many quarrels with our fists,
When 't was " Rush the blessed shack again," and
    " Strike the beggar back again,"
  And " If your man is clinching, break his wrists."

But 't was hell — pure hell — the way we did it.
  It was — " Up and burst your fellow if you can," —
The maids we used to walk about, the things we used
    to talk about,
  Are those which make a devil of a man.

So drink to what we 'll do, and what we 've finished,
  We 'll spend the money wildly as we wrought;
Let pious people chatter, why to them it does n't matter
  If we drop below the quarry face or not.
But they talk a little rot about our morals,
  And rave a little cant about our shame,
But, boys, they do not know of it, the trebly cursèd
    woe of it,
  'T is we who know, the players in the game.

And 't is hell — pure hell — and we have seen it,
  Our comrades dropping wildly off the slips,
When outworks broke to fall apart, when landslides
    shoved the wall apart,
  They died like men, with curses on their lips.

The lives that snapped in death, sure they 'll remind us
  Of the sorrow striking fiercely to the core,
The endless toil before us, the nameless graves behind
    us,
  Where our stricken comrades perished by the score.
These are the little facts that make us brutal,
  The things that make us curse above our breath,
The furious fight infernal, that is ours to wage
    eternal —
  The tragedy more horrible than death.

But it is n't in our power, my boys, to mend it,
  So we 'll face it to the final with a curse ;
But it 's hell — pure hell — until it 's ended.
  And ended — well — it — can — be — nothing —
    worse.

THE CONGER EEL

THE waters dance on the ocean crest, or swirl in
the cyclone's breath,
But down below where the divers go, they sullenly
sleep in death,
Where the slime is holding the cutter's stays, where
the sailors' bones are white,
Where the phantoms sweep through the eerie deep in
realms of endless night,
'T is there it holds its sway supine, and plaits its every
reel,
The silent, sibilant, sombre, sinuous, stealthy Conger
eel,
The silky Conger eel, the solemn-eyed Conger eel —
It circles by where the dead men lie, the spectral
Conger eel.

The devil fish, grim in its cavern dim, a sinister siren
lies,
And the shark will seize on its frightened prey where
the spumous surges rise,
The dolphin may play in its riotous way where the
waters are calm and slow,
The whale may spout like a geyser out by the ice of an
Arctic floe,
But down a hundred fathoms or more below the lance-
edged keel,
It slily slides, 'neath the shifty tides, the sensuous Con-
ger eel,

The lily-soft Conger eel, the green-eyed Conger eel,
It grovels in grime and the stagnant slime, the hideous
    Conger eel.

And there in its sluggish realms of woe it has reigned
    for unnumbered years.
It feasted of old on the vikings bold, and the Spanish
    buccaneers,
And kings and the sons of kings have gone to lie on its
    banquet board,
And many a lady young and fair from the arms of her
    drowning lord —
But down below no blush of shame comes to the lips
    that steal
The kisses soft from the lady fair; the passionless
    Conger eel
The cynical Conger eel, carnivorous Conger eel,
May lie on the breast of the maiden chaste and never
    a tremor feel —
That vampire Conger eel.

BACK FROM KINLOCHLEVEN

And the place that knew him, knows him no more.

THE waterworks are finished and the boys have
    jacked the shovel,
  See, the concrete board deserted, for the barrow squad
    is gone,
The gambling school is bursted, there is silence in the
    hovel,
  For the lads are sliding townwards and are padding
    it since dawn.
Pinched and pallid are their faces from their graft in
    God-shunned places,
  Tortured, twisted up their frames are, slow and lum-
    bering their gait,
But unto their hopeful dreaming comes the town with
    lights a-gleaming,
  Where the bar-men add more water, and the shame-
    less women wait.

Eighteen months of day shift, night shift, easy, slavish,
    long or light shift,
  Anchorites on musty bacon, crusty bread, and evil
    tea,
Sweated through the Summer till grim Winter came a
    hoary pilgrim,
  Chasing from the meagre blanket the familiar,
    flighty flea.[1]

[1] The wicked flea, that all men pursueth. — MOLES KIN JOE.

Then the days when through the cutting came the
    death-white snowflakes drifting,
  When the bar was chilled and frosted, and the
    jumper seared like hell,
When the hammer shook uncertain in the grimy hands
    uplifting,
  And the chisel bounced uncanny 'neath the listless
    strokes that fell.

But to Him give thanks 't is over and the city fills the
    distance,
  On the line of least resistance they are coming sure
    but slow,
How they wait the trull and harlot, jail-bird, vaga-
    bond and varlet,
  For there 's many a bob to squander and the city
    ravens know!
Parasites from pub and alley welcome in the grimed
    and greasy,
  Gather round with wail and plaudit, eager for their
    dough and gin,
They are coming from the muck-pile and they mean to
    take it easy,
  They have pals to share their joy and incidentally
    their tin.

They are tabid and outworn, unpresentable, unshorn,
  Occupants of many a model, wooers of the harridan,
Workers of the wildernesses, dressing as the savage
    dresses,
  Crawling in the rear of progress, following the
    march of man.
Where grim nature reigneth lonely over gelid places,
    only

Known to death and desolation, they have roughed
it long and hard,
Where the chronic river wallows in the refuse of the
hollows,
And the thunderbolt is resting on the mountain tops
it scarred.

But 't is over for the moment, and the heel-end of
creation
Vomits back the men who roughed it to the town
that sent them forth,
They who face the death it threatened with a grim
determination,
They who wrestled with the slayer incarnated in
the North —
Go and see them primed with lager, drain them of
the coppers sought for
In the depths of desolation, in the byways of the
beast,
Go and bum them of the ha'pence that like maniacs
they wrought for,
For they bear the famine bravely, but can never
stand the feast.

They are coming to the city, soon you'll see their
rants and quarrels,
See them marching off to prison, see them drinking
day by day,
In the dead end of their labours they forgot your code
of morals,
They are ne'er intoxicated in the super-saintly way.
You will know them by their reeking shag, you'll
know their way of speaking,

You can spot them by their moleskins and their
   bluchers battered down,
They are wild, uncultivated, maybe rather under-
   rated —
   But at any rate you'll know them by their curses
   when in town.

THE DEATH OF MOLESKIN

Here lies the remains of John Todd,
Not dead, but drunk, by God!
          — MOLESKIN.

JOE is dead? Of course he is,
    Dead as any nail can be,
Look upon that face of his —
    See, if you are sober, see
The unutterable peace
    Stamped upon his countenance —
See, and let your prattle cease,
    Give the dead man half a chance.

Joe is dead? Of course he 's dead;
    Hair dishevelled on his brow,
Lay him on the model bed,
    Nought avails to wake him now.
See, the jar is almost full —
    Look, I 've piles and piles of dough —
Moleskin, have another pull.
    Not an answer. Poor — old — Joe.

Give the fallen man his due,
    He was one that always could
Take a modest pint or two,
    Just as any navvy should,
Do a week or two in jile,
    Strike a bargain with a fence,
Fight his man in perfect style,
    Play the game, and stump the pence.

Poor old Joe is lying dead
　　Drunk as e'er a man can be,
Lay some lager near his head
　　So when waking he may see —
Softly let us go to sleep,
　　Be your voices hushed and low.
Hark his snoring loud and deep —
　　Peace be with your slumber, Joe.

CHOSES DU SOIR

(From the French of Hugo.)

CHILLY the eve, and the silent mist
　　Veils the moon in a mystic haze,
　　The cattle go down by the waterways,
And the skyline glimmers like amethyst.

A silhouette on the lonely dune
　　The traveller shows twixt earth and sky,
　　And fretfully cawing the rooks go by,
Shrinking in fright from the leprous moon.

The witch sits down, a ghoul at her throat,
　　And over the tarn the goblins call,
　　The spider has spun its web on the wall,
And waits for its prey and wearies not.

　　　This of old was thy song, Ivon —
　　　The song is living, the singer gone.

Apart the storm-chased luggers fly,
　　The straining mainmast is stripped and bare,
　　And the billows sing to the whirling air
A dirge for a failing dynasty.

The coach goes rumbling along the road,
　　The road that leads to the wide world's end,
　　Carrying, mother or wife or friend —
Pity the ones who to-night are abroad.

On the hillside lone the graveyard is,
  A cross, a flower, a written stone,
  The worm that crawls on the skeleton,
And the mouldering lips that we loved to kiss.

The fire is bright on the cottage hearth,
  The kettle sings in an undertone
  A song of joy that is all its own,
And children are full of idle mirth.

> *This of old was thy song, Ivon —*
> *Where is the wayward singer gone?*

THE SONG OF WERNER

(From the German of Scheffel.)

O ROMAN maid! why do you try
　　To win a heart you cannot hold
With honeyed word and witching eye?
　For ah! the ancient fire is cold.

Beyond the virgin Alpine snow,
　My lady sleeps beside the Rhine —
Upon her grave three roses blow,
　Her grave — who was the love of mine.

O, maid of Rome! you cannot move
　The heart that sorrow steeped in gloom;
For me alone but one to love,
　My lady sleeping in the tomb.

THE SLAVE

What mean ye that ye beat my people into pieces, and grind
the faces of the poor? — Isai. iii., 15.

THE olden chronicles tell us Akbar the slave was
    strong,
On the woes of his brothers in bondage he brooded and
    sorrowed long,
Akbar, the slave of Reienos, scarred with the iron and
    thong.

He toiled in the field and forest and furrow early and
    late,
Dragging through ruts and ridges, with slouching and
    servile gait;
But Akbar the slave was human, and Akbar the slave
    could hate.

Under the goad of the master, sweating as horses
    sweat,
Scorned by the page and lady appareled in satinet,
The sinewy slave could suffer, suffer and not forget.

. . . .

When the heat of the day was over and the tremulous
    stars looked wan,
When night hung low on the turret, drawbridge and
    barbican,
Into the darkling forest stealthily stole a man.

Silent as steals a panther, quick as a wolf on prowl,
A shadow among the shadows, almost unseen by the
   owl,
As the watch dog saw the figure in awe it filled the
   night with its howl.

In a hut in the depth of the thicket, rugged, misshapen,
   rude,
Akbar the slave of Reienos in the spiritless solitude,
With the cleverness hate had given, fashioned a slab
   of wood.

The prong of a graip for a gimlet, a sharpened spade
   for a plane,
He shapened it level and specular, smooth as the shield
   of a thane,
Toiling alone in the darkness, filled with a passion
   insane.

With withes of the seasoned willows he tied it as firm
   as steel
Down to the bench in the dwelling, filled with a giant's
   zeal,
Then made he with maniac labour a grim and horrible
   wheel.

With the rim of flexible pinewood, the lissome fir for
   the spoke,
A groove and a rope around it, a turning handle of
   oak,
Thus Akbar spoke in the darkness, timing his ham-
   mer's stroke —

" The brutes of the byres are tended, there is food for
    the hunting pack,
He has trampled the crumbs from his table, the crumbs
    that my brothers lack,
Reienos has tortured and lashed us — now I will pay
    him back.

" Lord, I have waited to see Thee strike him down in
    his crime,
I who am nearly outworn, whipped like a cur in my
    prime,
Vengeance is Thine it is spoken, but I cannot abide
    Thy time."

    .   .   .   .

The arrogant Lord Reienos strode through the woods
    alone,
Far through the gloomy forest thinking of things
    unknown,
Reienos the strong and fearless, hard of heart as a
    stone.

As a panther hangs on its quarry, as a vulture circles
    afar,
A sinister figure followed, silent as moves a star,
Akbar, the grim avenger, marked with the sear and
    the scar.

The rubescent sun sank westward, tingeing with ver-
    meil dyes,
The shimmering leaves of the forest, the gentian dome
    of the skies,
And showing the tigerish hate in the villein's passion-
    ate eyes.

H

A crash in the brake behind him, like when a boar
    breaks through —
Reienos turned in anger, turned, and saw, and knew —
And the slayer laughed in the silence for the deed he
    lusted to do.

Laughed and laid hold of his master, gripped him
    fiercely and strong —
Seized like a leaf in the cyclone, borne as a straw is
    along,
Reienos thought on his Maker, Akbar remembered the
    thong.

In the zest of the whirlwind foray Reienos had led
    the way,
When the noise of the shields and spears rang to the
    vault of day,
But death at the hands of a villein — Reienos began
    to pray.

Into the gloomy cabin drear as the pit of dread,
Down on the slab he placed him, his hands above his
    head,
Tied to the wheel, his body fastened with withe and
    thread.

" Pray to heaven for mercy as your hours are almost
    done,
The lowly slave at your castle may look on the mor-
    row's sun,
But two will pass ere it rises, and thou, Reienos, art
    one —

" One, and I am the other — strung from your castle
wall —
Pray — I have prayed for years outside your lordly
hall,
But God in Heaven was busy watching the sparrows
fall."

.   .   .   .

Flaxen pale the moonshine glimmered on dune and
tree,
A groan came borne on the breezes, lone and piteously,
A wheel is turned in the cabin, a maniac laughs in glee,

A meteor streaks the impearled dome with its fiery
light,
Cluster on cluster they sparkle stars that are diamond
bright,
Another turn in the torture, another moan in the
night.

Falling as falls the spice flower adown the mane of the
breeze,
Slowly the molten moonfire fell on the bearded trees,
Where the eerie midnight vampires bowed at their
fetishes.

Borne in dismal cadence, the groans of the sufferer
Sank away in the silence, died on the midnight air,
And only the grim avenger watched by the body
there.

They found the slave in the dawning, beside the lord
of the hall,

They hung him in scorn and fury, high from the castle
    wall,
The man who wept for his people, the man who tired
    of his thrall.

.   .   .   .

Only an ancient story, fraught with its weight of woe,
Of the love of a slave for freedom, and the hate that
    crushed him low —
Only an outworn story, now — as in long ago.

A GEOLOGICAL NIGHTMARE

THE lurid volcanoes were guarding the pole,
   The sinister flames reached the Northern star —
I wandered through ages untold with my soul
   And the grim fellowship of the plesiosaur,
In the regions of felspar and red syenite,
   Where the mammoth was romping in furious glee,
Where the ichthyosaur chased the slim belemnite,
   Through the lava-tinged waves of a Triassic sea.

On the clubmoss I saw the wild dinosaur feed,
   From the primeval tree swung the anthropoid ape,
Through the network of fern and cyad and reed
   Crashed the long brontosaur of the cumbersome
     shape;
The grim armadillo that wallowed in slime,
   The lizard and serpent that flew in the air,
Looked weird in that eerie pre-adamite time
   'Neath the luminous sun or the stellary bear.

   .   .   .   .

But where are they gone to, the mammoth and auk?
   The dodo and dragon — say, where are they gone?
In the Triassic beds and the Eocene chalk
   They have fallen asleep and are slumbering on.
The knight of the sickle has numbered their days,
   And Nature embalmed them in shells and in stones,
And we their descendants in boundless amaze,
   Discuss them, or pore on their fossilized bones.

Thus *we* even pass from the gentian dome,
   And follow the trail of the monsters that saw
The heaven of stars that ne'er glimmered on Rome,
   Adown to the vale of ineffable awe —
We go with the pallor of fear on our face,
   They went from the fight with the bloodstain and
     scar,
And the man and the maiden must rest in the place
   Where they wait them the dragon and ichthyosaur!

THE PIONEER

HE was a servant boy, and he
Married a maid of his own degree,
Rented a plot of the mountain lands,
And faced the wild with willing hands,
Where the whortleberry and monkshood grew,
And the night-shade steeped in the poison dew.
The juniper covered the rocky ledge,
The bramble grew to the torrent's edge;
The meadow land was rough and damp,
With here a rock and there a swamp;
The pines came flocking around his door;
The cold spring oozed through the cabin floor,
But, save for his wife, companionless,
He raised his hands to the wilderness.

The pine went down before his axe,
The scanty corn grew up in his tracks,
With shovel and spade the mead was drained,
With weary labour the brook was chained,
With his simple faith, and two men's power,
A giant he wrought through sun and shower,
And of every yard he dared dispute
With the wild, it drove him back a foot,
For its ways are many, its strength is great,
And man is conquered soon or late.

The woman died in a twelvemonth's space,
And left him alone in the gloomy place;
But sorrowful, silent, yet unsubdued,
He delved and drilled and hammered and hewed,

Clearing the brambles, breaking the stones,
Till the fever set in his aching bones,
And the jeering wraith of the wild in wrath
Flung him in scorn from out its path.

Then the corn rotted, the drain fell low,
Again the bramble began to grow,
The sapling grew by the fallen log,
And he died in his hut as dies a dog,
Shivering, thirsty, afraid, alone,
Unhappy, uncared for, and unknown. * * *
This is the story fraught with fear,
The tale of the rustic pioneer.

After him came the mine and mill,
A city was built upon the hill;
There bearded fools in the council sat,
And jabbered their views upon this and that,
But no one knew or cared to hear,
The tale of the early pioneer.

THE HOUSE OF REST

UNTO a land unknown to me I came on some
  strange mission sent,
 A lonely pilgrim from the night I wandered on a
  wonder way,
And said, " I 'll seek athrough the world for rest and
  unalloyed content,"
 And sought beneath the frigid stars, and sought be-
  neath the fretful day.

I saw the House of Toil, and there the people died for
  lack of bread,
 There gnawing hunger kept her rule relentless o'er
  the battered roof,
And in the House of Love they wept for spoken words
  and words unsaid —
 I gripped my staff in mute despair and firmly kept
  myself aloof.

The House of Wealth was fair to see, all damascened
  and diapered,
 But inside riot reigned supreme, and sated men had
  blighted health,
While outside gaunt-eyed forms went by, and starving
  children's cries were heard,
 And godless ones with sinful souls crept in and ran-
  sacked it by stealth.

The House of God was passing grand, with moulded
  arch and sculptured door,
  With picture, psalter, pulpit, pew, with printed
  prayer and priceless pyx,
But from within an endless wail was wafted upwards
  evermore,
  And hair was rent and sackcloth worn beneath the
  silent crucifix.

The House of Azreel stands alone, and greater than
  abyssmal night
  The gloom of it, and depth of it, unruffled by the
  softest breath —
The door is ope, I enter there, and dressed in robes of
  pallid white,
  I greet the worm, and rest me in the House of
  Azreel and of Death.

And here where never mellow morn may send a ray
  of light or bliss,
  Where never lingering winds are borne, where never
  maiden's voice is heard,
Afar from holiness and hate, from kindness and the
  soulless kiss,
  I sleep content for endless years and never wish to
  speak a word.

THE OLD MEN

THERE 'S a handful of meal in the barrel, and a
   little oil in the cruse,
We wear out our thin-soled sandals, they tan for the
   next year's shoes,
And whet their axe at the grindstone, while ours hangs
   blunt on the wall,
And willingly shapen the rooftree, though ours is ready
   to fall.
The old fleece rots on the wether, the new fleece whirls
   in the loom,
They weave the cloth for the bridal, we fashion the
   shroud for the tomb,
Who followed the path as we found it from dawn to
   decline of day,
Till the great world lies behind us, before us the
   lonely way.

Our sons go into the forest, our sons go out to the
   mead,
And labour with saw or with sickle, everyone unto his
   need,
Our daughters will meet them at even, with smile and
   with simper and sigh,
And the love that their mothers bore us, in days that
   have drifted by;
On their lips the red blood crimsons, and their golden
   tresses glow,
But we 've seen the red lips whiten and the tresses turn
   to snow.

What makes us envy the moments they snatch from the
    swift-winged fate,
And the fury that follows after, catching them soon or
    late?
Some fierce inherent hatred the brute of the wilderness
    bore
As he lost command of the wolfpack when young and
    swift no more,
Some olden envious instinct the hoary chieftain had
When the reins of his despot power passed to a beard-
    less lad;
Ours is the useless prattle, the solace of Solomon,
When he loathed the maids of his harem, and the days
    of his lusts were gone,
With the scorn of the young to goad us, and the doom
    that dogs our feet,
We are the olden cynics, wise in our own conceit.

There's a handful of meal in the barrel, and a little
    oil in the cruse,
Which our toothless loves will bake us — we who are
    little use —
Let our sons go out to the hunting, let our daughters
    simper and smile;
We wait for the welcome summons — only a little
    while,
For we are the useless old men, wrinkled and bent and
    grey,
With the things we have done behind us, before us
    the lampless way;
We are the useless old men with faltering, failing
    breath,
With a stake in the great Hereafter, sealed by the
    hand of Death.

THE END

GAUNT clouds are piled athwart the sky,
　The cold wind soughs along the earth,
In hapless towns the people die,
　The fires are cold on every hearth,
The spectral moon has lost its light,
　The shrunken sun is pale and wan,
And time is one unholy night —
　A night that never knows a dawn.

Forsaken homes where mortals dwelt
　Are drear as death and still as Styx,
The cloisters where the godly knelt
　Are fallen on the crucifix;
No watcher ponders on the stars,
　Of life and death no sages tell,
No soldier hastens to the wars,
　No preacher speaks of heaven or hell.

The fiery meteors cross the skies,
　And far apart the Twins have gone,
A planet to the sacrifice!
　And Paris sleeps with Babylon.
A mighty race has passed away,
　A fretful planet whirled in space —
A pawn in time's unending play,
　Is mourning for the mighty race.

" NO MORE "

(Written on the evictions in Gweedore on the northern coast of Ireland.)

THE sun moves on its path of light
   Across the heaven's floor,
The welkin beams above the night —
   But they return no more.

The mountains sentinel the glen
   And all its emerald store,
The meadow, copsewood, and the fen —
   But they return no more.

The honeysuckle in the vale
   Was ne'er so fair before,
The roses scent the evening gale —
   But they return no more.

The watchdog, waiting hollow-eyed
   Before the cabin door,
No more will be the peasant's pride,
   For they return no more.

For ever stilled the evening latch,
   The peat fire's glow is o'er,
The ivy fattens on the thatch,
   For they return no more.

The ocean twines its throbbing arms
  Around the silent shore,
Or raises loud its wild alarums —
  But they return no more.

Upon the beach the lugger lies
  Beside the useless oar,
No more 't will bear the fisher's prize,
  Now they return no more.

Where once the weaver plied his trade
  The shuttle's flight is o'er,
The ditch now holds the rotted spade,
  And they return no more.

Not now is heard the evening chime,
  The reapers' song is o'er,
They wander weary in a clime
  From which they come no more.

Sad, sad, thy tale, land of my birth,
  Bear witness wild Gweedore,
Thy children banished o'er the earth,
  And they return no more.

SALVE, REX DEI GRACIA!

This may have happened in new-world times,
    Or yet in the ages of long ago,
I am a writer writing my rhymes,
    And how on earth should a rhymer know!

THERE lived a man who was wise and old,
    And the old are wise, we must all agree,
And the things he had learned were manifold,
For he ate the fruit of the knowledge tree.
But lo, and behold you! there came to him,
As he walked abroad in the city square,
Scholar and merchant and soldier grim,
Who making obeisance spoke him fair: —

" We come, from the people of many a land,
Unworthy to press your garment hem —
To crown thee here, as is their command,
For the sake of the good you have done for them.
We come from the peoples of town on town,
The people, who know your power and worth,
And they bade us bring you a golden crown
And crown you — the greatest man on earth."

" We slept, and you toiled thro' the lee-long night,
You saw us unmeet, and made us fit."
But the brow of the seer grew black as night;
And he questioned—"What merit has come of it?
I have planned the ships that ye sail afar,
And taught you to sharpen the arrow-head;
But your ships are battered in shiftless war,
And your brothers' blood on the arrow is red.

" I have taught you to build your houses fine;
But the beggars grovel before the door,
And you house your servants amongst the swine,
And boast your pride to the starving poor.
Now do you come with cant and crown
To crown me greatest of all mankind!
But, follow me far from the crowded town,
I 'll shew you the man you come to find!"

They followed him, far from the city square,
Soldier and scholar in cloak and hood.
They came to a village, the pump and there
Gaping the village idiot stood.
Untutored, unmeet to labour or plan,
A brainless, brutish and simple thing —
But the seer outspoke — " Behold the man
You claim as Monarch!   Go, crown him King!"

" King!" said the scholar, and laughed his mirth.
" King!" said the soldier, and loudly swore.
" Though long we have bowed to your power and
          worth,
Henceforth we scoff at your simple lore.
The good he has done, we would wish to hear
In town or in country, in forge or farm."
" Oh, little, perchance," replied the seer,
" But he never has done a mortal harm."

So the village idiot was crowned as King.
'T is strange, and in sooth it may be so.
I am a singer trying to sing,
And how on earth should a singer know?

I

DOWN ON THE DEAD END

(On tramp, 1909.)

I 'VE toiled at the end of creation, stripped to the
trousers and shirt,
I 've hashed like the very damnation and squandered
my money like dirt,
And jobs that are nameless I 've wrought in, and deeds
that are shameless I 've done,
And fights without number I 've fought in, and paid
like the deuce for my fun.

I 've piled up the slush in the bucket, down to my
knees in the drift,
Wet till I felt I must chuck it, or drop like a mule at
my shift,
In dreary and desolate places, with the boss standing
glowering by
At his men and their fungous-white faces, I 've felt as
if ready to die.

Drink, and I 've tried to keep from it, women and
cards — 't was the same,
The dog will return to his vomit, the devil is boss of
the game,
The red of the wine cup has hidden the adders with
poisonous teeth,
The sunlight is bright on the midden, with the rot of
the wide world beneath.

Disheartened, discarded, disgusted, I'm down on the dead-line once more,

Beggared, benighted and bursted, the jail or the workhouse before —

Well, life had its trouble and worry, the Fates have been devilish hard,

My chances went by in a hurry, I plunged on the rottenest card.

I haven't a pipe-full of Carroll's to cheer me while tramping it out,

And getting because of my morals a hell of a knocking about,

— Well! life was a foolhardy gamble and down in its by-ways I strove,

And perhaps in the ultimate scramble I'll corner a shakedown above.

RUN DOWN

IN the grim dead end he lies, with passionless filmy
    eyes,
  English Ned, with a hole in his head,
Staring up at the skies.

The engine driver swore as often he swore before —
  " I whistled him back from the flamin' track,
An' I could n't do no more."

The gaffer spoke through the 'phone " Platelayer
    Seventy-one
  Got killed to-day on the six-foot way,
By a goods on the city run.

    " English Ned was his name,
      No one knows whence he came,
    He did n't take mind of the road behind
      And none of us is to blame."

    They turned the slag in the bed
      To cover the clotted red,
  Washed the joints and the crimsoned points,
      And buried poor English Ned.

        In the drear dead end he lies,
        With the earth across his eyes,
          And a stone to say,
          How he passed away
        To a shift beyond the skies.

WITH THE BREAKDOWN SQUAD

" Wreck of the city express, sir,"
The newspaper sellers yell,
The people are buying, buying,
My! don't the papers sell,
And the publishers say in their usual way
" Business is doing well."

" **A** TANNER down on a three spot,
Losing again, he blowed! "
" Give me a fill of tobacco."
" Here, a one that I owed."
" Losing again with — Heavens!
A passenger off the road! "

Seventy-nine was the engine,
Speediest on the line —
We rushed to the van like demons
And waited the signal sign,
Then flashing afar like a scymitar
Went the flame of seventy-nine.

Out in the night as phantoms,
Out to the wreck we steal,
Horror urging our heart-beats,
Feeling as sinners feel —
The rails like souls in torment
Whimpered beneath the wheel.

Above us the moon went sailing
  White as the face of death,
Watching the engine gliding
  Over the world beneath,
While we pulled at our pipes in silence,
  And heard our every breath.

The engine fire is cleaving
  A path to the stars on high —
The cirrus clouds in the heaven
  Like burial shrouds go by,
Sent from the dim hereafter
  For men and women who die.

In the gaunt and gelid cutting
  Ghouls of the darkness brood,
A lone, belated raven
  Cries through the solitude,
And the signals rise to danger
  Redder than human blood.

A crash of brakes in the darkness —
  A rush and a crash again:
Men are wailing in anguish,
  Women laugh in their pain —
As a prayer that 's prayed by a grave new made
  Is the groan of the coupling chain.

The rails are splashed with crimson,
  There 's blood on the catcher bar,
The writhing engine hisses
  Through the sky-roofed abattoir —
As the flame in a midnight churchyard
  Is the light of each chilly star.

" Out with the lint and bandage —
  See are the stretchers spread —
Out with a man to the signal
  And guard the line ahead.
Haste, and look to the living
  Before you bother the dead.

There 's sorrow deeper than tears
  That words in vain may speak —
The tearless mother watches
  The red on her baby's cheek,
And downcast unwet lashes
  Tell of the hearts that break.

Out in the night and the horror
  We labour and curse or pray,
" Give me a drink of water — "
  " I 'll meet her some other day — "
We place the maimed on the stretchers,
  The dead in the six-foot way.

" Two inches wide in the gauging,
  Out with the ramps and — yes,
The facing points must have done it —
  Lord, what an awful mess!
But hurry and have it ready
  For passing the night express."

" *Awful railway disaster,*"
  The newspapers chronicle —
The men in the streets are buying —
  Gracious! the papers sell,
And the publishers say in their usual way
  " *Business is doing well.*"

ON THE LATE SHIFT

Mayhap there's a hitch in the signal wire,
  Or the other points are drawn,
But some go out on the night-shift lone
  That never come in with the dawn,
And a crimson splash on the engine wheel
  Just tells of the shunter gone.

SEVEN waggons to siding four, one to the buffer
    end —
  Damn you, watch! or they'll run you down.　God,
    it's a hellish night!
Jimmy Collins is getting a wife — time he was making
    a bend —
  There he's there at the dead-end points, signalling
    with the light.

" A good man out on the night-shift, Jim, willing —
    and ain't it queer,
  There he's singing, the first time I've heard him
    in my life —
Yes, willing and straight is Jimmy, I've mated him
    seven year —
  Damn it, it's blowing somewhat — and now he
    looks for a wife.

" See and look to your carcass, and watch!　On a night
    like this
  You never can tell the minute — where has that
    Collins gone ? —

An engine punches your ticket — God, if your feet
  should miss —
  Damn me! I think I'm nervous — signal the en-
  gine on.

   .   .   .   .

" Two o'clock! I was certain 't was almost break of
  day —
  Where is Collins? Oh, yonder. I'm wet to the
  very spine —
A train for the cross-road siding — pull it the other
  way —
  Collins, you fool! what ails you? Jump to the
  other line!

" Collins, you idiot, jump it! . . . Christ, he's down
  like a sack! . . .
  Surely he must have heard me. . . . Speak to me,
  Jimmy, do.
. . . Tell me you are n't hurted — ah! the blood on
  track —
  . . . I shifted the engine, Jimmy, but heavens! I
  thought you knew."

   .   .   .   .

" Break it to her in the morning — I was thinking
  about her, then —
  The wind was blowing awful — sudden the engine
  came. . . .
. . . Whistle the box for the signal. . . . Married to
  her at ten.
  . . . Father, who art in Heaven, hallowed be Thy
  name."

Mayhap there's a hitch in the signal wire,
Or the other points are drawn,

But a red stain gleams on the deadly flange,
And a night-shift man is gone —
And the bride to be has changed her robe
For a mourning dress at dawn.

A LAST WISH

(From the German of Sturm.)

WHEN my heart has ceased for ever beating out
the dirge of time,
Lay me by some quiet river, 'neath the ivy spray and
thyme,
Place no fading, fragrant roses, o'er the dew-be-
sprinkled moss,
For the weary sleeper chooses but the evergreen and
cross.

DREAMINGS

THE bog blossom's golden pistil,
  The shimmering torrent's crystal
Fling of its sapphire waters, crested with foam-drift
 white,
  The moorland and scent of the musky
  Wild flower borne on the dusky
Wings of the wandering breezes that carry the starry
 night,

  Come with dreams of the wondrous olden
  Times, when fancy's golden
Wand lay o'er my boyhood, filling my mind with
 joy —
  I can see the moor and the dimly
  Waving gorse, and grimly
The strong man smiles at the yearning that made the
 life of the boy.

  Ghosts of the olden faces,
  Voices from silent places,
Eyes that are filled with laughter, eyes that with tears
 are wet,
  Into the days so gloomy
  Come in my musings to me —
One who has ne'er forgotten, one who can ne'er forget.

MATER DOLOROSA

HE raised the latch iv his father's door,
    An' went, the dark look on his face —
I wait an' wait him ivermore,
On him I wait for ivermore,
    As not a wan can fill his place.

The kine go east at dawn iv day,
    In the cold grey dawn I tell my beads,
But out in the wurl' an' miles away,
An' miles an' miles so far away
    My Fergus lives an' niver heeds.

The kine come back to me at eve,
    But still he never comes anigh;
Through all the night I pray an' grieve,
Through all the long, black night I grieve,
    An' pray to God, an' cry an' cry.

An' "Mary pity me," I pray,
    I pray to God, "Thy will be done,"
But more to her my prayers I say,
To Mary, Mother, more I say,
    For long ago she lost her Son.

I look in the fire an' think an' sing,
    An' sing the songs he liked to hear,
An' often to my mind I bring
His form an' face, so well I bring,
    I think that he is very near.

I weep thro' all the lonely night,
  An' pray an' pray upon my knees,
That maybe with the morrow's light
He 'll come back, with the morrow's light —
  For Mary, Mother, hears an' sees.

UNFULFILLED

THERE is dew upon the meadows brightly glanc-
    ing in the morn,
And a blush of softest crimson comes across the wav-
    ing corn,
And the waters brightly gleaming journey onward to
    the sea,
But nought fulfils the promise that the Springtime
    made to me.

'T is the olden, olden story, with its hope and with
    its pain,
Loved awhile with deep devotion, never to be loved
    again —
Oft again will gentle Springtime paint the flower
    and tint the tree,
But the soft-voiced Spring will never bring its
    second hopes to me.

Oft will mem'ry's fairy musings light upon the past
    again,
Ere the spell of love was broken by the alchemy of
    pain —
We were young, and we were happy, trusting in the
    future — we —
But the present 's full of sorrow, and the sorrow falls
    on me.

There is dew upon the meadows brightly glancing in
the morn,
And a crimson blush of promise rises on the waving
corn,
And the earth with hope is pregnant; howsoever it
may be,
It can ne'er fulfil the promise that the Springtime
made to me.

THE VALLEY

A FAIRY-LIKE valley, with grim mountains
    hiding it,
Peacefully sleeping 'mong meadow-lands fair,
A river of carmine and silver dividing it,
    And scent of the wild-flowers filling the air.
Never a grey mist comes earthwards enshrouding it,
    There never weepeth the cypress or yew,
Only the night-shadows lovingly clouding it,
    Or trellised cirrus with stars peeping through.

Up by the braes, there the heather bells cluster,
    Where the wind-flower blooms and the gorse-blos-
        soms be
Guarding the lane, see the bright daisies muster
    The starry battalions by hedgerow and tree.
Over the sedges a streamlet is flinging its
    Frivolous waters in vermeil-tinged spray,
Over the fallow a wild bird is singing its
    Song of delight to the ears of the day.

A woodland is there and the blackberries grow in it,
    And grey gnarled oaks that the ages have bent,
Blossoms as white and as pure as the snow in it,
    Fair as the stars in the deep firmament.
A shadowy pool where the green water-cresses are
    Languidly floating in sensuous rest,
Is hidden 'mid ferns that with tremulous tresses are
    Playing with glee in the breath of the west.

K

A valley of dreams, with the dim mountains hiding it,
   Streamlets of silver through meadow-lands fair,
A river of carmine and sapphire dividing it,
   And scent of the wild flowers filling the air.

A TALE OF THE BOGLAND

'T IS meself that hates the city, an' the hurry, an'
    the din —
An' I wish that I was out of it, its worry an' its sin,
For me mind is on the bogland, when the day is drear
    an' dim;
I could be happy all me life, if I was back with him.
But the wurl is up agin' me, an' so bitter is me heart,
For he is on the bogland yet, an' I am far apart.

'T is meself that loved the bogland stretchin' out agin'
    the sky,
With the summer flowers a-blowin' an' the peat-stacks
    gettin' dry;
There was dew upon the heather at the dawnin' o' the
    day,
An' the rushes in the marshes ever sung their sleepy
    lay,
An' he told me in the gloamin' that I won his manly
    heart,
But he is on the bogland yet, an' I am far apart.

'T is meself that loved to linger when the big red sun
    went down,
An' the purple heavens rested on the bogland lone
    an' brown;
I told him when I met him that I loved the evenin'
    air,
Tho' glorious the evenin' well I knew he would be
    there,

An' he loved me with devotion, an' he pressed me to
    his heart,
But he is on the bogland yet, an' I am far apart.

'T is meself regrets the hour that I met the stranger
    there,
But he had got a manner fine an' such a pleasant air;
He told me of the wonder sights an' glories of the
    town
Until me eyes grew weary of the bogland's waste of
    brown,
But though the strangers' halls are fine, mine is a
    broken heart,
For he is on the bogland yet, an' I am far apart.

LONGINGS

(Burns model lodging-house, 1910.)

THERE is clatter on the pavement, there is hurry
    in the street,
  The curtains of the night are dropping down,
The heart-throbs of the city clang with dull insistent
    beat,
  The gas lights glimmer faintly thro' the town —
The ten-hour shift is laboured, and the gaffer's voice
    is still,
  And my thoughts go o'er the ocean surge afar,
To the meadow and the river and the boreen and the
    hill,
  And the little lime-washed cottage in Kilcar.

I have seen the crimson dawning of a Spanish morn-
    ing glow,
  I have cowered before the menace of the wild,
I have seen the sapphire sunlight tint the everlasting
    snow
  Where December's virgin granaries are piled,
I have heard the mountain torrents hurtle riotous in
    wrath,
  I have tramped the roads to London and to Rome,
But I'd rather have my childhood and the narrow
    moorland path,
  The path that leads to happiness and home.
I am sitting by the hot-plate and my comrades talk
    about
  The things they've done and which they shouldn't
    do,

I have been their pal in sinning, and I 've got to grin
        it out,
    And the harvest of my oats is overdue —
'T is not so much the slaving in the sewerage of life,
    'T is not so much the toiling and the wet,
'T is not so much the curbing of my hatred of the
        strife,
    But the shattered dreams I never can forget.

The shrines the world has broken were the shrines
        at which I knelt,
    And the faith I cherished so it laughed to shame,
But God alone in Heaven knows the sufferings I felt,
    When I sold my youth's ideals for a name,
And pawned my simple virtues for a meed of evil
        praise,
    Ah, I pledged them where I never could redeem,
Tho' to many it was merely just a love of newer ways,
    To me it was the waking from a dream.

They are rough and rugged fellows, my companions
        sworn and true,
    And maybe I am rough and rude as they —
But oh, heavens! how they 'd mock me, if by chance
        they ever knew
    That I hankered for a cabin miles away —
Where it stands above the shingle that the waters
        whirl upon,
    As they race across the sandhill and the bar —
That I long for it by night, dreaming by the hot-plate
        bright,
    My father's homely cottage in Kilcar.

GOING HOME

(Doherty's shack, 1909.)

I'M going back to Glenties when the harvest fields
  are brown,
And the Autumn sunset lingers on my little Irish
  town,
When the gossamer is shining where the moorland
  blossoms blow
I 'll take the road across the hills I tramped so long
  ago —
'T is far I am beyond the seas, but yearning voices call,
" Will you not come back to Glenties, and your wave-
  washed Donegal ? "

I 've seen the hopes of childhood stifled by the hand of
  time,
I 've seen the smile of innocence become the frown of
  crime,
I 've seen the wrong rise high and strong, I 've seen
  the fair betrayed,
Until the faltering heart fell low, the brave became
  afraid —
But still the cry comes out to me, the homely voices
  call,
From the Glen among the highlands of my ancient
  Donegal.

Sure, I think I see them often, when the night is on
  the town,
The Braes of old Strasala, and the homes of Carrig-
  doun —

There 's a light in Jimmy Lynch's house, a shadow on
    the blind,
I often watched the shadow, for 't was Mary in be-
    hind,
And often in the darkness, 't is myself that sees it all,
For I cannot help but dreaming of the folk in Donegal.

So I 'll hie me back to Glenties when the harvest comes
    again,
And the kine are in the pasture and the berries in the
    lane,
Then they 'll give me such a handshake that my heart
    will leap with joy,
When a father and a mother welcome back their way-
    ward boy.
So I 'm going back to Glenties when the autumn
    showers fall,
And the harvest home is cheery in my dear old
    Donegal.

THE RETURN

THE boy came home from a foreign land,
    Weary and wan, with his staff in hand;
Five years' absence had left their trace
On golden hair, and on sunny face.
His gait was weary, his limbs were sore;
His youthful friends knew him no more.
The grey-haired padre passed him by
Unrecognised. With a heedless eye
The toll gatekeeper saw him pass and go
Up the dusty road, but in years ago,
The boy was the dearest friend he had,
But the tollman's eyes with the years grew bad.
As fair as of old 'neath her summer hat,
At the cottage door his sweetheart sat,
But the white dust rose from the road on high,
And she knew him not as he passed her by.
He entered his home with footsteps slow —
His friends forgot him, would his parents know?
" God bless you, stranger," the father cries,
But the sun shone strong in the old man's eyes.
But the mother wept on his neck with joy —
" My son, my son, my wandering boy."

HOME

I'M back again in Glenties and the Autumn wind
      is blowing,
The silver-sandalled evening skips across the moun-
      tains high,
But the bogland flowers are fading where of old I
      watched them growing,
And the lean leaves of Lammas tide are whirling thro'
      the sky.

The bogland flowers are fading, and I mark them as
      a token
Of the early hopes I cherished to my sorrow and re-
      gret;
The silver cord is loosened, and the golden bowl is
      broken,
And another heart is wearisome and longing to forget.

The slender threads of gossamer are shining on the
      heather,
The little brooks are tumbling as they hurry to and
      fro,
I tramp along the boreen that we tramped of old
      together,
My love and I together in the days of long ago.

The road across the moorland sure it's twisting an'
      it's turning
Round the braes of old Strasala and the heights of
      Carrigdoun,

But in the mellow Autumn dusk one lamp has ceased
    from burning,
And a hearth is cold and cheerless on the way to
    Glenties town.

I 'll leave my home again and I 'll bid good-bye to-
    morrow,
And I 'll pass the little churchyard and the tomb
    a-near the wall,
I have lived so much for love I can hardly live for
    sorrow
By the grave that holds my colleen in a glen of
    Donegal.

THE DEPARTED

DOWN from the open spaces where the banshee
wails to the moon,
From the lonely moorland places where the witches
hold domain,
Like a ghost of the past the midnight blast wails at my
window pane,
Out of the night and the silence it comes to my window
pane,
      Full of a longing vain
It has wafted thro' her burial shroud, and the matted
coils of her hair,
Where the ghouls of the gloom foregather over the
tomb wherein
She moulders away to the senseless clay — she who
was free from sin.
Heaven! the grave and its horrors, ugly and dark as
sin,
      And the beautiful maid therein!

Sunlight and moonlight and starlight, interblent with
the dew,
The modesty of the passion flower, the youthful, hope-
ful glow —
She was greater to me than the world to be, than any-
thing mortals know,
Greater by far than life or death, or aught that the
mortals know
      In this evil-starred world below.

And the weeping wind in the darkness lingers around
her tomb,
Presses her clay cold tresses and lips where my lips
have lain,
And I hear it say in its wistful way — When do we
meet again?
When do you meet your olden love and keep your
tryst again?
Says the wind at the window pane.

HEROES

What is a man? Not ours to ask,
  Not ours to make reply.
But from Southampton to the Clyde
  Can Britain testify —
That they are men and more than men
  Who know the way to die.

THE little blue fox has seen it break apart from
    the riven floe,
The little blue fox of the Arctic waste that seeks its
    food in the snow;
On gale-gored beach and wave-washed cliff the bear
    has seen it reel,
The polar bear as it left its lair to hunt for the frozen
    seal.
The lone moose bull on some outcast cape has won-
    dered to see it pass,
As it shuffled the snow off its feeding grounds and
    sought for the meagre grass.

The sealer scurried from out its track, and the fright-
    ened whaler fled,
For the derelict berg on the fishing seas is a thing of
    fear and dread.
'T was battered and worn by icy waves and swept by
    their madd'ning wrath,
And the Northern Lights came out at night to glare
    on its lonely path.

But ever and on 'neath the dusk and dawn to the
  southern seas it bore,
With the lean locked lands of the north astern and
  the trackless seas before.

. . . .

Proudly she swung from the crowded pier, as the
  mooring chains ran free,
Virgin pure from the Belfast docks, to the olden trail
  of the sea.
As the music swelled from the fading beach, the
  pounding screws replied,
And the grey, lank waves went gliding by, an arm's
  reach overside.
Alas! for the joy of the lover and maid, alas! for the
  children gay —
The little blue fox on the Arctic waste is safer by
  far than they.

. . . .

West! and the English fields grew dim, and the coast-
  wise lights shone clear.
Say, did they laugh on the crowded decks, and the
  doom so very near?
West! and the coastwise lights gave out, and the stars
  of heaven shone,
And the sailor watched through the midnight hour,
  aloof, apart, alone.

South! 'neath the sinister polar star the death-bearing
  berg went forth.
Oh! they who sail on herded seas should dread the
  Doom of the North.
May Heaven pity the sailor man, when the Northern
  Doom's abroad,
For the ship is built by the human hand, the berg by
  the hand of God.

The stars looked down from the lonely sky — as they
    looked on the polar snow
Where the bear had eaten the little blue fox it killed
    by the Arctic floe.

.   .   .   .

Say, was the joke in the stateroom heard, the laugh
    on the maiden's lips?
Lord of the waves! have pity on men who go down to
    the sea in ships.
Say, did the grimy stoker smile in the heat of the fur-
    nace breath?
We do not know, but this we know, he laughed in
    the face of Death.
Say, did the lover hurry and fret to come to his sweet-
    heart's side?
We only know, when the davits swung, he gallantly
    stood aside.
And some there were, whose life and work was much
    misunderstood,
But in the hour that tried their souls, we know their
    death was good.
And greater by far than deeds of war or right or a
    grand mistake
Is a life that is given in sacrifice for a child or a
    woman's sake.

What is a man? Not ours to ask,
    Nor yet to make reply.
But from Southampton to the Clyde
    Can Britain testify
That they are men and more than men
    Who know the way to die.

THE OLD LURE

(Fleet Street, 1912.)

WHEN the gaunt night covers the city,
    And the fog drifts down the wind,
I sit in my study thinking
    Of the pals I left behind;
And the old lure of the old life
    Enters into my mind.

I 'm sick of the books before me,
    And the sorry lore that they hold;
And I long for the full-blooded lusty youth,
    That passed like a tale that 's told.
Oh! the old life is the sweetest life;
    And my heart goes back to the old

Dibble and drift and drill,
    Ratchet and rail and rod,
Shovel and spanner and screw,
    Hard-hafted hammer and hod,
The rattle of wheels on the facing points,
    And the smell of the rain-washed sod.

The call of a wondrous past
    Is throbbing in my heart-strings,
The danger-lights aflare
    Where the hooded signal swings,
The clash of the closing blades,
    As the straining point-rod springs.

L

The old friend is the best friend,
  He who has stood the test:
The old song is the sweetest song,
  Sweeter than all the rest.
And the old life that I left behind
  Is far and away the best.

When I go back to the old pals,
  'T is a glad, glad boy I 'll be;
With them will I share the doss-house bunk,
  And join their revels with glee;
And the lean men of the lone shacks
  Shall share their tucker with me.

My hobnailed bluchers I shall put on,
  Firm in welt and vamp,
And get me moleskin and corduroy,
  Proof to the dirt and damp,
And sweat on the shift with the navvy-men
  And doss again with the tramp.

Where the sunsets flame on the offside track
  Amber and cochineal,
Where the dawn breaks, a waking rose,
  I 'll beg and starve and steal,
Or hash with the stiff-lipped navvy-men,
  And feel as I used to feel.

'T is oh! for the hot-plate reeking red,
  When the naphtha lamps are lit,
As the jokes go round the gambling school
  Told with a ready wit,
The well-won rest of a slavish day,
  The joy and glamour of it!

Sick indeed of the city am I,
   Its make-believe and its show,
The roar and rush of the crowded streets
   Where men run to and fro.
For I 've hashed in the drift for seven year,
   And back to the drift I 'll go,
Back to the men of the lone lank lands
   And the pals of long ago.

THE LAST RHYME, SAVE ONE

I have gathered a posie of other men's flowers, and nothing
but the thread that binds them is mine own. — MONTAIGNE.

I 'VE sung in a wayward fashion
  The song of a rugged heart,
With less of power than of passion,
  With more of desire than art,
Tales of roving and roaming,
  Stories of daring done,
While ye wait for the poet coming —
  The singer of later on.

From drear and deserted places,
  Where the wastes of creation lie,
Where the pitiless hail-cloud races
  Over the merciless sky,
On the offside of desolation
  When the fog is fetid and dense,
In the watchman's reeking station
  Guarding the sliprail fence,
Tales of the great unholy,
  Lazily, lovingly, long,
I 've gathered in byways lowly
  And fashioned them into song.

The rime of the roving fellow
  Who dreams by the midnight fire,
When the autumn leaves are yellow
  And sere as his youth's desire.

The dirge of the loosened boulder
　And the thing that gasps beneath,
While the hod is yet on the shoulder,
　The pipe is yet in the teeth,
Of the dynamite in the boring,
　That did n't go off when it should,
And the pick that went exploring,
　And the pal who left for good —
For ever the signal reddens,
　For ever is danger near,
And the sound of the up-train deadens
　The down-train's roar in the ear.

　.　　.　　.　　.　　.　　.　　.

Thus have I sung their story,
　That wondrous story of theirs,
The navvies' sorrow and glory,
　And death that is unawares,
But under the rougher singing,
　In a quivering undertone,
Perchance you will hear it ringing,
　A song that is all mine own,
Out of its rough environs,
　The roar of the running cars,
The lilt of the canting irons,
　The rune of the lifting bars,
Apart from the navvy quarrels,
　Card-school riot and song,
Manners, merits and morals,
　And chivalry — going wrong —
Perchance that you will discover
　Under the rugged art
The voice of the nature lover,
　The song of the singer's heart.

A poet will follow after,
A poet of later years,
To sing of their joy and laughter,
And weep for their woe and tears,
Striking the tuneful lyre
Greater than me by far,
As the rose outrivals the briar,
As the sun outrivals the star,
And the songs I sing in the gloaming
May turn to nought in the dawn
That beams for the singer coming,
The poet of later on.

L'ENVOI — TO MY PICK AND SHOVEL

*When the last, long shift will be laboured, and the
    lying time will be burst,*
*And we go as picks or shovels, navvies or nabobs,
    must,*
*When you go up on the scrap-heap and I go down
    to the dust,*

Will ever a one remember the times our voices rung,
*When you were limber and lissome, and I was lusty
    and young?*
*Remember the jobs we've laboured, the heartful songs
    we've sung?*

*Perhaps some mortal in speaking will give us a kindly
    thought —*
*" There is a muck-pile they shifted, here is a place
    where they wrought."*
*But maybe our straining and striving and singing will
    go for nought,*

*When you go up on the scrap-heap, and I go down
    to the dust —*
*(Little children of labour, food for the worms and
    the rust,)*
*When the last long shift will be laboured and the
    lying time will be burst.*

SOLDIER SONGS

My dear H. J.,

You have often asked me what
are the favourite songs of the soldier on
Active Service, the rhymed lines which
give expression to his soul. It is difficult
to give an answer, the mere words are
" dud " shells, which drop harmlessly to
earth close to their objective. The
soldier and his song cannot be separated
from their surroundings.

Let me explain and quote in illustra-
tion an incident which occurred a few
weeks ago.

A certain regiment, which glories in
the name of the " Old Diehards," sent a

7

draft to the "London Irish," and the new-comers attached to our battalion became part of the units' fighting strength. Sixty per cent of the draft were "old sweats," men who had fought well on many a bloody field, and added by prowess of arms numerous honours to their own beloved regiment. They had shared their last crust with hearty comrades in the retreat from Mons, they battled side by side with these comrades on the Marne, and wept over their graves by the Aisne.

The circumstances of war strengthen the *esprit-de-corps* of a soldier, and I am not far wrong in stating that pride of regiment in an "old sweat" is much stronger than love of country. On the evening of their arrival these veterans sat in their huts and sang the song of the " Old Diehards." Mere doggerel the verse, the words fatuous, and the singing not above reproach. But the song touched the hearts of the audience ; the listeners were " old sweats " who had songs of their own.

As I listened I thought of the children of Israel, who hung their harps on the willows and mourned for Babylon. The feeling engendered in a man when a futile shell drops close to him and fails to explode is difficult to make manifest in cold words ; but it is even more difficult to give an adequate idea of the impression created in the hearts of those who listened to the song of the " Old Diehards." The soldiers have songs of their own, songs of the march, the trench, the billet and battle. Their origin is lost ; the songs have arisen like old folk-tales, spontaneous choruses that voice the moods of a moment and of many moments which are monotonously alike. Most of the verse is of no import ; the crowd has no sense of poetic values ; it is the singing alone which gives expression to the soldier's soul. " Tipperary " means home when it is sung in a shell-shattered billet, on the long march " Tipperary " is Berlin, the goal of high emprise and great adventures.

Let me speak of a few songs which we sing. This is our idea of the peace which may follow our years of war.

" When the war is over
  We're going to live in Dover,
  When the war is over we're going to have a spree,

We're going to have a fight
In the middle of the night
With the whizz-bangs a-flying in the air."

Though we cannot picture a peace which will be in no way associated with high explosives, we can dream in the midst of the conflict of the desirable things that civil life would bring us.

What time we waited for Kitchener's Army in Flanders and lost all hope of ever seeing it, this song was sung up and down the trenches by the Territorials and Regulars.

" Who are the boys that fighting's for,
   Who are the lads to win the war,
   It's good old Kitchener's Army.
   And every man of them's très bon,
   They never lost a trench since Mons,
   Because they never saw one."

Here are a few others which have echoed in billets and dug-outs from Le Harve to the Somme, and which have accompanied the wild abandon of drinking nights in Poperinghe and Bethune.

THE SOLDIER'S LETTER

" I've lost my rifle and bayonet,
I've lost my pull-through too,
I've lost the socks that you sent me
That lasted the whole winter through,
I've lost the razor that shaved me,
I've lost my four-by-two,
I've lost my hold-all and now I've got damn all
Since I've lost you."

SING ME TO SLEEP

Sing me to sleep where bullets fall,
Let me forget the war and all ;
Damp is my dug-out, cold my feet,
Nothing but bully and biscuits to eat.
Over the sandbags helmets you'll find
Corpses in front and corpses behind.

Chorus.

Far, far from Ypres I long to be,
Where German snipers can't get at me,
Think of me crouching where the worms creep,
Waiting for the sergeant to sing me to sleep.

Sing me to sleep in some old shed,
The rats all running around my head,
Stretched out upon my waterproof,
Dodging the raindrops through the roof,
Dreaming of home and nights in the West,
Somebody's overseas boots on my chest.

The Tommy is a singing soldier ; he sings to the village patronne even when ordering food, and his song is in French.

" Voulez vous donnez moi
      Si'l vous plaît
      Pain et beurre
      Et café au lait."

He serenades the maiden at the village pump.

" Après la guerre fini
Soldat Anglais partee,
M'selle Frongsay boko pleury,
Après la guerre fini."

The soldier has in reality very few songs ;
he has many choruses which get worth
from the mood that inspires them and the
emotions which they evoke.   None will
outlast the turmoil in which they origin-
ated ;   having   weathered   the   leaden
storms of war, their vibrant strains will
be choked and smothered in atmospheres
of Peace.   " These 'ere songs are no good
in England," my friend Rifleman Bill
Teake remarks.   " They 'ave too much
guts in them."

When I said I wanted to dedicate
" Soldier Songs " to you I did not then
anticipate inflicting upon you so lengthy

a dedicatory letter ; but when writing of the men of the British armies, old and new, I find it difficult to be concise.

Yours,

PATRICK MACGILL.

Lammas Day, 1916.

CONTENTS

B   17

CONTENTS

CONTENTS

AFTER LOOS

(Café Pierre le Blanc, Nouex les Mines, Michaelmas Eve, 1915.)

WAS it only yesterday
Lusty comrades marched away ?
Now they're covered up with clay.

Seven glasses used to be
Called for six good mates and me—
Now we only call for three.

Little crosses neat and white,
Looking lonely every night,
Tell of comrades killed in fight.

23

Hearty fellows they have been,

And no more will they be seen

Drinking wine in Nouex les Mines.

Lithe and supple lads were they,

Marching merrily away—

Was it only yesterday ?

THE OLE SWEATS

(*1st Birmingham War Hospital, Ruberry, Birmingham.*)

WE'RE goin' easy now a bit, all dressed in
blighty blue,*

We've 'eld the trenches eighteen months and
copped some packets too,

We've met the Boches on the Marne and fought
them on the Aisne,

We broke 'em up at New Chapelle and 'ere we
are again.

The ole sweats—

All that is left of the ole sweats.

More went away than are with us to-day.

Gawd ! but we miss 'em, the ole sweats.

* Hospital uniform.

25

And now that we've a blighty one* we don't
    know what to do !—

Just swing the lead ; the Darby boys will see
    the bisness through,

They'll 'ave a bit o' carry on, o' fightin' and o'
    fun,

They'll 'ave the ribbons when they end the
    work that we begun.

        The ole sweats—

    Devils for fun were the ole sweats,

    In love or a scrap sure they always went nap,

    They 'adn't 'arf guts had the ole sweats.

But the old sweats they never die, they only
    fade away

And others come to take their place, 'ot on
    the doin's they ;

* A blighty one. A wound which brings a soldier back to
England.

They're drillin' up from day to day, at it at
    dusk and dawn,

But they'll need it all to fill the shoes of blokes
    that now are gone ;

       The ole sweats,

    The ole daisy-shovers,* the ole sweats.

  The new 'uns it's said they are smart on
    parade,

    But, Gawd, there is none like the ole sweats.

We're out 't for duration now and do not care
    a cuss,

There's beer to spare at dinner time and afters †
    now for us,

But if our butty's still were out in Flanders
    raisin' Cain,

We'd weather through with those we knew on
    bully beef again.

---

  * Daisy-shovers.   The dead ; "the men who lie under the
ground, shoving the daisies up with their toes."
  † Afters = confiture.

The ole sweats—

The grub it was skimp with the ole sweats.

But if rashuns was small 'twas the same for
us all,

Same for the 'ole of the ole sweats.

Well, if you want a sooveneer, a bit of blighty
blue,

There's empty tunic sleeves to spare, a trousers
leg or two,

And some day when you see us stand on
Charing Cross parade,

Present a boot before us just to 'elp us at our
trade.

The ole sweats—

Tuppence a shine with the ole sweats.

So you'll give us a show when you see us, we
know,

Us that is left of the ole sweats.

LA BASSEE ROAD

(Cuinchy, 1915.)

You'll see from the La Bassée Road, on any
  summer's day,

The children herding nanny-goats, the women
  making hay.

You'll see the soldiers, khaki clad, in column
  and platoon,

Come swinging up La Bassée Road from billets
  in Bethune.

There's hay to save and corn to cut, but harder
  work by far

Awaits the soldier boys who reap the harvest
  fields of war.

You'll see them swinging up the road where
  women work at hay,

The straight long road,—La Bassée Road,—on
  any summer day.

29

The night-breeze sweeps La Bassée Road, the
  night-dews wet the hay,
The boys are coming back again, a straggling
  crowd are they.
The column's lines are broken, there are gaps
  in the platoon,
They'll not need many billets, now, for soldiers
  in Bethune,
For many boys, good lusty boys, who marched
  away so fine,
Have now got little homes of clay beside the
  firing line.
Good luck to them, God speed to them, the
  boys who march away,
A-singing up La Bassée road each sunny
  summer day.

A LAMENT

(*The Ritz-Loos Salient.*)

I WISH the sea were not so wide
    That parts me from my love ;
I wish the things men do below
    Were known to God above.

I wish that I were back again
    In the glens of Donegal,
They'll call me coward if I return,
    But a hero if I fall.

" Is it better to be a living coward,
    Or thrice a hero dead ? "
" It's better to go to sleep, my lad,"
    The Colour Sergeant said.

31

THE GUNS

(Shivery-shake Dug-out, Maroc.)

THERE'S a battery snug in the spinney,

    A French seventy-five in the mine,

A big nine-point-two in the village

    Three miles to the rear of the line.

The gunners will clean them at dawning

    And slumber beside them all day,

But the guns chant a chorus at sunset,

    And then you should hear what they say.

Chorus.

Whizz bang! pip squeak! ss-ss-st!

Big guns, little guns waken up to it.

We're in for heaps of trouble, dug-outs at

    the double,

And stretcher-bearers ready to tend the

    boys who're hit.

32

And then there's the little machine-gun,—

  A beggar for blood going large.

Go, fill up his belly with iron,

  And he'll spit in the face of a charge.

The foe fixed his ladders at daybreak,

  He's over the top with the sun ;

He's waiting ; for ever he's waiting,

  The pert little vigilant gun.

Chorus.

  Its tit-tit ! tit-tit ! tit ! tit ! tit !

  Hark the little terror bristling up to it !

  See his victims lying, wounded sore and
        dying—

  Red the field and volume on which his name
        is writ.

The howitzer lurks in an alley,

  (The howitzer isn't a fool,)

c

With a bearing of snub-nosed detachment

    He squats like a toad on a stool.

He's a close-lipped and masterly beggar,

    A fellow with little to say,

But the little he says he can say in

    A most irrepressible way.

Chorus.

    OO—plonk ! OO-plonk ! plonk ! plonk !
        plonk !

    The bomb that bears the message riots
        through the air.

    The dug-outs topple over on the foemen
        under cover,

    They'll slumber through revelly who get
        the message there !

The battery barks in the spinney,

    The howitzer *plonks* like the deuce,

The big nine point two speaks like thunder

   And shatters the houses in Loos,

Sharp chatters the little machine-gun,

   Oh ! when will its chattering stop ?—

At dawn, when we swarm up the ladders ;

   At dawn we go over the top !

Chorus.

Whizz bang ! pip squeak ! OO-plonk ! sst !

Up the ladders ! Over ! And carry on
   with it !

The guns all chant their chorus, the shells
   go whizzing o'er us :—

Forward, hearties ! Forward to do our
   little bit !

THE NIGHT BEFORE AND THE NIGHT
AFTER THE CHARGE

On sword and gun the shadows reel and riot,
  A lone breeze whispers at the dug-out door,
The trench is silent and the night is quiet,
  And boys in khaki slumber on the floor.
    A sentinel on guard, my watch I keep
    And guard the dug-out where my
      comrades sleep.

The moon looks down upon a ghost-like figure,
  Delving a furrow in the cold, damp sod.
The grave is ready and the lonely digger
  Leaves the departed to their rest and God.
    I shape a little cross and plant it deep
    To mark the dug-out where my com-
      rades sleep.

36

IT'S A FAR, FAR CRY

It's a far, far cry to my own land,
 A hundred leagues or more,
To moorlands where the fairies flit
 In Rosses and Gweedore,
Where white-maned waves come prancing up
 To Dooran's rugged shore.

There's a cabin there by a holy well,
 Once blessed by Columbcille,
And a holly bush and a fairy fort
 On the slope of Glenties Hill,
Where the dancing feet of many winds
 Go roving at their will.

37

My heart is sick of the level lands,

    Where the wingless windmills be,

Where the long-nosed guns from dusk to dawn

    Are speaking angrily ;

But the little home by Glenties Hill,

    Ah ! that's the place for me.

A candle stuck on the muddy floor

    Lights up the dug-out wall,

And I see in its flame the prancing sea

    And the mountains straight and tall ;

For my heart is more than often back

    By the hills of Donegal.

OFF DUTY

THE night is full of magic, and the moonlit
    dewdrops glisten
Where the blossoms close in slumber and the
    questing bullets pass—
Where the bullets hit the level I can hear them
    as I listen,
Like a little cricket concert, chirping chorus in
    the grass.

In the dug-out by the traverse there's a candle-
    flame a-winking
And the fireflies on the sandbags have their
    torches all aflame.
As I watch them in the moonlight, sure, I
    cannot keep from thinking,
That the world I knew and this one carry on
    the very same.

39

Look ! A gun flash to the eastward ! " Cover,
    matey ! Under cover !

Don't you know the flash of danger ? You
    should know that signal well ;

You can hear it as it's coming. There it passes ;
    swooping over.

There's a threat of desolation in the passing of
    a shell."

Little spears of grass are waving, decked with
    jewels iridescent—

Hark ! A man on watch is stricken—I can
    hear his dying moan—

Lies a road across the starland near the wan
    and waning crescent,

Where a sentinel off-duty goes to reach his
    Maker's Throne.

I OFT GO OUT AT NIGHT-TIME

I OFT go out at night-time
    When all the sky's a-flare
And little lights of battle
    Are dancing in the air.

I use my pick and shovel
    To dig a little hole,
And there I sit till morning—
    A listening-patrol.

A silly little sickle
    Of moon is hung above ;
Within a pond beside me
    The frogs are making love :

41

I see the German sap-head ;
A cow is lying there,
Its belly like a barrel,
Its legs are in the air.

The big guns rip like thunder,
The bullets whizz o'erhead,
But o'er the sea in England
Good people lie abed.

And over there in England
May every honest soul
Sleep sound while we sit watching
On listening patrol.

THE CROSS

(On the grave of an unknown British soldier,
Givenchy, 1915.)

THE cross is twined with gossamer,—

    The cross some hand has shaped with care,

And by his grave the grasses stir

    But he is silent sleeping there.

The guns speak loud : he hears them not ;

    The night goes by : he does not know ;

A lone white cross stands on the spot,

    And tells of one who sleeps below.

The brooding night is hushed and still,

    The crooning breeze draws quiet breath,

A star-shell flares upon the hill

    And lights the lowly house of death.

Unknown, a soldier slumbers there,

   While mournful mists come dropping low,

But oh ! a weary maiden's prayer,

   And oh ! a mother's tears of woe

THE TOMMY'S LAMENT

(The Ritz–Loos Salient.)

I FANCY it's not 'arf my chance
    To go on plodding 'neath my pack,
Parading like a snail through France,
    My house upon my bloomin' back.

My wants are few, but what I need
    Ain't not so much of bully stew,
Nor biscuits, that's a mongrel's feed,
    But, matey, just 'twixt me and you—

When winks the early evening star,
    And shadows o'er the trenches come—
I wish the sergeants brought a jar,
    And issued double tots of rum.

MARCHING

(La Bassée Road, June, 1915.)

FOUR by four, in column of route,
By roads that the poplars sentinel,
Clank of rifle and crunch of boot—
All are marching and all is well.
White, so white is the distant moon,
Salmon-pink is the furnace glare
And we hum, as we march, a ragtime tune,
Khaki boys in the long platoon,
Ready for anything—anywhere.

Lonely and still the village lies,
The houses sleep and the blinds are drawn,
The road is straight as the bullet flies,
And we go marching into the dawn ;

Salmon-pink is the furnace sheen.

Where the coal stacks bulk in the ghostly air

The long platoons on the move are seen,

Little connecting files between,

Moving and moving, anywhere.

IN FAIRYLAND

THE field is red with poppy flowers,
　　Where mushroom meadows stand ;
It's only seven fairy hours
　　From there to Fairyland.

Now when the star-shells riot up
　　In flares of red and green,
Each fairy leaves her buttercup
　　And goes to see her queen.

Where little, ghostly moonbeams stray
　　Through mushroom alleys white,
The fairies carry on their way
　　A glow-worm lamp for light.

48

For them the journey's always short ;

   They're happy as you please,

A-riding to the Fairy Court

   On backs of bumble-bees.

The cricket and the grasshopper

   Are thridding in the grass,

And making paths of gossamer

   For fairy feet to pass.

Whene'er I see a glow-worm light

   In Boyau* seventeen,

I know the fairies go that night

   To see the Fairy Queen.

* French communication trench.

D

I HAVE a big French rifle, its stock is riddled
 clean,
And shrapnel-smashed its barrel, likewise its
 magazine.
I've lugged it from Bethune to Loos and back
 from Loos again,
I've found it on the battlefield amidst the
 soldiers slain.
A little battle souvenir for one across the foam
That's if the French authorities will let me
 take it home.

I've got a long, long sabre as sharp as any
 lance,

'Twas carried by a shepherd boy from some-
    where South in France

Where grasses wave and poppy-flowers are red
    as blood is red.

I took the shepherd's sabre for the shepherd
    boy lay dead.

I'll take it back a souvenir to one across the
    foam

That's if the French authorities will let me
    take it home,

That's if our own authorities will give me leave
    for home ! ! !

BEFORE THE CHARGE

(Loos, 1915.)

THE night is still and the air is keen,
　　Tense with menace the time crawls by,
In front is the town and its homes are seen,
　　Blurred in outline against the sky.

The dead leaves float in the sighing air,
　　The darkness moves like a curtain drawn,
A veil which the morning sun will tear
　　From the face of death.—We charge at dawn.

LETTERS

(*Vermelles, August*, 1915.)

WHEN stand-to hour is over we leave the
parapet,

And scamper to our dug-out to smoke a
cigarette ;

The post has brought in parcels and letters for
us all,

And now we'll light a candle, a little penny
candle,

A tiny tallow candle, and stick it to the wall.

Dark shadows cringe and cower on roof and
wall and floor,

And little roving breezes come rustling through
  the door ;
We open up the letters of friends across the
  foam,
And thoughts go back to London, again we
  dream of London—
We see the lights of London, of London and of
  home.

We've parcels small and parcels of a quite
  gigantic size,
We've Devon cream and butter and apples
  baked in pies,
We'll make a night of feasting and all will have
  their fill—
See, cot-mate Bill has dainties, such dandy,
  dinky dainties,

She's one to choose the dainties, the maid
    that's gone on Bill.

Oh : Kensington for neatness ; it packs its
    parcels well,

Though Bow is always bulky it isn't quite as
    swell,

But here there's no distinction 'twixt Kensing-
    ton and Bow,

We're comrades in the dug-out, all equals in
    the dug-out,

We're comrades in the dug-out and fight a
    common foe.

Here comes the ration party with tins of bully
    stew—

" Clear off your ration party, we have no need
    of you ;

" Maconachie for breakfast ? It ain't no
    bloomin' use,
We're faring far, far better, our gifts from
    home are better,
Look here, we've something better than bully
    after Loos."

The post comes trenchward nightly ; we hail
    the post with glee,
Though now we're not as many as once we
    used to be,
For some have done their fighting, packed up
    and gone away,
And many boys are sleeping, no sound will
    break their sleeping,
Brave lusty comrades sleeping in little homes
    of clay.

We all have read our letters, but one's un-
        touched so far,

An English maiden's letter to her sweetheart
        at the War,

And when we write in answer to tell her how
        he fell,

What can we say to cheer her ? Oh, what is
        now to cheer her ?

There's nothing left to cheer her except the
        news to tell.

We'll write to her to-morrow and this is what
        we'll say,

He breathed her name in dying ; in peace he
        passed away—

No words about his moaning, his anguish and
        his pain,

When slowly, slowly dying. God ! Fifteen
hours in dying !
He lay a maimed thing dying, alone upon the
plain.

We often write to mothers, to sweethearts and
to wives,
And tell how those who loved them have given
up their lives ;
If we're not always truthful, our lies are always
kind,
Our letters lie to cheer them, to solace and to
cheer them,
Oh : anything to cheer them,—the women left
behind.

THE EVERYDAY OF WAR

(Hospital, Versailles, November, 1915.)

A HAND is crippled, a leg is gone,
 And fighting's past for me,
The empty hours crawl slowly on ;
 How they flew where I used to be !
Empty hours in the empty days,
 And empty months crawl by,
The brown battalions go their way,
 And here at the Base I lie !

I dream of the grasses the dew-drops drench,
 And the earth with the soft rain wet,
I dream of the curve of a winding trench,
 And a loop-holed parapet ;

59

The sister wraps my bandage again,
　　Oh, gentle the sister's hand,
But the smart of a restless longing, vain,
　　She cannot understand.

At night I can see the trench once more,
　　And the dug-out candle lit,
The shadows it throws on wall and floor
　　Form and flutter and flit.
Over the trenches the night-shades fall
　　And the questing bullet pings,
And a brazier glows by the dug-out wall,
　　Where the bubbling mess-tin sings.

I dream of the long, white, sleepy night
　　Where the fir-lined roadway runs
Up to the shell-scarred fields of fight
　　And the loud-voiced earnest guns ;

The rolling limber and jolting cart

   The khaki-clad platoon,

The eager eye and the stout young heart,

   And the silver-sandalled moon.

But here I'm kept to the narrow bed,

   A maimed and broken thing—

Never a long day's march ahead

   Where brown battalions swing.

But though time drags by like a wounded snake

   Where the young life's lure's denied,

A good stiff lip for the old pal's sake,

   And the old battalion's pride !

The ward-fire burns in a cheery way,

   A vision in every flame,

There are books to read and games to play

   But oh ! for an old, old game,

With glancing bay-net and trusty gun

    And wild blood, bursting free !—

But an arm is crippled, a leg is gone,

    And the game's no more for me.

THE LONDON LADS

(While standing to arms in billets, La Beuvriere,
July, 1915.)

ALONG the road in the evening the brown
    battalions wind,
With the trenches' threat of death before, the
    peaceful homes behind ;
And luck is with you or luck is not as the ticket
    of fate is drawn,
The boys go up to the trench at dusk, but who
    will come back at dawn ?

The winds come soft of an evening o'er the
    fields of golden grain,
The good sharp scythes will cut the corn ere we
    come back again ;

The village girls will tend the grain and mill the
    Autumn yield
While we go forth to other work upon another
    field.

They'll cook the big brown Flemish loaves and
    tend the oven fire,
And while they do the daily toil of barn and
    bench and byre
They'll think of hearty fellows gone and sigh
    for them in vain—
The billet boys, the London lads who won't
    come back again.

THE LITTLE BROWN BIRD

THERE'S a little brown bird in the
    spinney,
  With a little gold cap on its head,
Gold as the gold of a guinea,
  And its legs they are wobbly and
    red.

MYSELF. " Little brown bird, is your singing
    Over and finished and done ? "
BIRD.   " I wait for the fairy who's bringing
    Spring and its showers and its sun."

MYSELF. " What will you do in December ? "
BIRD.   " Do ? What I'm doing just now :
    Here on the first of November,
    Shivering mute on a bough."

MYSELF. " But April will find you quite

cheery ! "

I said with a pang in my breast.

BIRD.   " In April I'll get me a dearie

And help her to fashion a nest "

THE LISTENING-PATROL

WITH my bosom friend, Bill, armed ready to
    kill,
  I go over the top as a listening-patrol.
Good watch we will keep if we don't fall asleep,
  As we huddle for warmth in a shell-shovelled
    hole.

In the battle-lit night all the plain is alight,
  Where the grasshoppers chirp to the frogs
    in the pond,
And the star-shells are seen bursting red, blue,
    and green,
  O'er the enemy's trench just a stone's-throw
    beyond.

The grasses hang damp o'er each wee glow-
worm lamp

That is placed on the ground for a fairy
camp-fire,

And the night-breezes wheel where the mice
squeak and squeal,

Making sounds like the enemy cutting our
wire.

Here are thousands of toads in their ancient
abodes,

Each toad on its stool and each stool in its
place,

And a robin sits by with a vigilant eye

On a grim garden-spider's wife washing her
face.

Now Bill never sees any marvels like these,

When I speak of the sights he looks up with
amaze,

And he smothers a yawn, saying, " Wake me at
    dawn,"
  While the Dustman from Nod sprinkles dust
    in his eyes.

But these things you'll see if you come out
    with me,
  And sit by my side in a shell-shovelled hole,
Where the fairy-bells croon to the ivory moon
  When the soldier is out on a listening-patrol.

A VISION

THIS is a tale of the trenches
  Told when the shadows creep
Over the bay and traverse
  And poppies fall asleep.

When the men stand still to their rifles,
  And the star-shells riot and flare,
Flung from the sandbag alleys,
  Into the ghostly air.

They see in the growing grasses
  That rise from the beaten zone
Their poor unforgotten comrades
  Wasting in skin and bone,

And the grass creeps silently o'er them

    Where comrade and foe are blent

In God's own peaceful churchyard

    When the fire of their might is spent.

But the men who stand to their rifles

    See all the dead on the plain

Rise at the hour of midnight

    To fight their battles again.

Each to his place in the combat,

    All to the parts they played

With bayonet, brisk to its purpose,

    Rifle and hand grenade.

Shadow races with shadow,

    Steel comes quick on steel,

Swords that are deadly silent

    And shadows that do not feel.

And shades recoil and recover

And fade away as they fall

In the space between the trenches,

And the watchers see it all.

A.D. 1916

THE sky shows cold where the roof has been,
But the stars of night are none the dimmer,
Where the home once stood are the ruins seen,
But the brazier glows with a cheery glimmer,
And the old life goes and the new life fills
The scenes of many a peasant story,
And the bursting shells on the sentried hills
Whisper of death but shout of glory !

Gutted and ripped the stricken earth,
Where the bones of the restless dead are
        showing ;
But the great earth breathes of life and birth,
And ruin shrinks from the blossoms blowing.

73

The old life fails, but the new life comes

Over the ruins scarred and hoary,

Though the thunder of guns and the roll of

    drums

But make for death while they shout of glory.

THE HIPE

" WHAT do you do with your rifle, son ? " I
    clean it every day,
And rub it with an oily rag to keep the rust
    away ;
I slope, present, and port the thing when
    sweating on parade.
I strop my razor on the sling ; the bayonet
    stand is made
For me to hang my mirror on. I often use it,
    too,
As handle for the dixie, sir, and lug around the
    stew.
" But did you ever fire it, son ? " Just once,
    but never more.

I fired it at a German trench, and when my
  work was o'er
The sergeant down the barrel glanced, and
  then he said to me,
" Your hipe* is dirty. Penalty is seven days'
  C.B. ! "

* Hipe, regimental slang for a rifle.

THE TRENCH

THE long trench, twisting, turning, wanders
    wayward as a river
  Through the poppy-flowers blooming in the
    grasses dewy wet,
The buttercups sit shyly and the daisies nod
    and quiver,
  Where the bright defiant bayonets rim the
    sandbagged parapet,
In the peaceful dawn the trenches hold a
    menace and a threat.

The last faint evening streamer touches heaven
    with its finger,
  The vast night's starry legion sends its first
    lone herald star,

Around the bay and traverse little twilight
colours linger
And incense-laden breezes come in crooning
from afar,
To where above the sandbags gleam the steely
fangs of war.

All the night the frogs go chuckle, all the day
the birds are singing
In the pond beside the meadow, by the
roadway poplar-lined,
In the field between the trenches are a million
blossoms springing
'Twixt the grass of silver bayonets where the
lines of battle wind
Where man has manned the trenches for the
maiming of his kind.

ON ACTIVE SERVICE

FOR the bloke on Active Service, w'en 'e goes
    across the sea,

'E's sure to stand in terror of the things 'e
    doesn't see,

A 'and grenade or mortar as it leaves the other
    side

You can see an' 'ear it comin', so you simply
    steps aside.

The aeroplane above you may go droppin'
    bombs a bit,

But lyin' in your dug-out you're unlucky if
    you're 'it.

W'en the breezes fills your trenches with
    hasfixiatin' gas,

You puts on your respirator an' allows the
stuff to pass.

W'en you're up against a feller with a bayonet
long an' keen,

Just 'ave purchase of your weapon an' you'll
drill the beggar clean.

W'en man and 'oss is chargin' you, upon your
knees you kneel,

An' catch the 'oss's breastbone with an inch
or two of steel.

It's sure to end its canter, an' as the creature
stops

The rider pitches forward an' you catch 'im as
'e drops.

It's w'en 'e sees 'is danger, an' 'e knows 'is way
about

That a bloke is damned unlucky if e's knocked
completely out.

But out on Active Service there are dangers
   everywhere,

The shrapnel shell and bullet that comes on
   you unaware,

The saucy little rifle is a perky little maid,

An' w'en you've got 'er message you 'ave done
   your last parade.

The four-point-five will seek you from some
   distant leafy wood,

An' taps you on the napper an' you're out of
   step for good.

From the gun within the spinney to the sniper
   up a tree

There are terrors waitin' Tommy in the things
   'e doesn't see.

F

BILLETS

OUR old battalion billets still,

Parades as usual go on,

We buckle in with right good will

And daily our equipment don

As if we meant to fight, but no !

The guns are booming through the air,

The trenches call us on, but oh !

We don't go there, we don't go there !

At night the stars are shining bright

The old world voice is whispering near,

We've heard it when the moon was light,

And London's streets were very dear ;

But dearer now they are, sweetheart,

The buses running to the Strand,—

But we're so far, so far apart,

Each lonely in a different land.

But, dear, with sentiment aside

(The candle dwindles to the cheese*)

I wish the sea were not so wide

When distance brings such thoughts as these.

One glance to see the foreign sky,

One look to note the stars o'erhead,

Sweet thoughts to you, sweetheart, and I

Turn in to billet barn, and bed.

* The Old Sweats fashion sconces from cheese.

IN THE MORNING

(Loos, 1915.)

THE firefly haunts were lighted yet,

    As we scaled the top of the parapet ;

But the East grew pale to another fire,

    As our bayonets gleamed by the foeman's
      wire ;

And the sky was tinged with gold and grey,

    And under our feet the dead men lay,

Stiff by the loop-holed barricade ;

    Food of the bomb and the hand-grenade ;

Still in the slushy pool and mud—

    Ah ! the path we came was a path of blood,

      When we went to Loos in the morning.

84

A little grey church at the foot of a hill,

  With powdered glass on the window-sill.

The shell-scarred stone and the broken tile,

  Littered the chancel, nave and aisle—

Broken the altar and smashed the pyx,

  And the rubble covered the crucifix ;

This we saw when the charge was done,

  And the gas-clouds paled in the rising
    sun,

    As we entered Loos in the morning.

The dead men lay on the shell-scarred plain,

  Where Death and the Autumn held their
    reign—

Like banded ghosts in the heavens grey

  The smoke of the powder paled away ;

Where riven and rent the spinney trees

  Shivered and shook in the sullen breeze,

And there, where the trench through the
  graveyard wound,
    The dead men's bones stuck over the ground
      By the road to Loos in the morning.

The turret towers that stood in the air,
  Sheltered a foeman sniper there—
They found, who fell to the sniper's aim,
  A field of death on the field of fame ;
And stiff in khaki the boys were laid
  To the sniper's toll at the barricade,
But the quick went clattering through the
  town,
    Shot at the sniper and brought him down,
      As we entered Loos in the morning.

The dead men lay on the cellar stair,
  Toll of the bomb that found them there.

In the street men fell as a bullock drops,

   Sniped from the fringe of Hulluch copse.

And the choking fumes of the deadly shell

   Curtained the place where our comrades fell,

This we saw when the charge was done

   And the East blushed red to the rising sun

      In the town of Loos in the morning.

TO MARGARET

IF we forget the Fairies,
And tread upon their rings,
God will perchance forget us,
And think of other things.

When we forget you, Fairies,
Who guard our spirits' light :
God will forget the morrow,
And Day forget the Night.

DEATH AND THE FAIRIES

BEFORE I joined the Army
I lived in Donegal,
Where every night the Fairies
Would hold their carnival.

But now I'm out in Flanders,
Where men like wheat-ears fall,
And it's Death and not the Fairies
Who is holding carnival.

THE RETURN

THERE's a tramp o' feet in the mornin,'
There's an oath from an N.C.O.,
As up the road to the trenches
The brown battalions go :
Guns and rifles and wagons,
Transports and horses and men,
Up with the flush of the dawnin',
And back with the night again.

Back again from the battle,
From the mates we've left behind,
And our officers are gloomy
And the N.C.O.'s are kind ;

When a Jew's harp breaks the silence,

Purring an old refrain,

Singing the song of the soldier,

" Here we are again ! "

Here we are !

Here we are !

Oh ! here we are again !

Some have gone west,

Best of the best,

Lying out in the rain,

Stiff as stones in the open,

Out of the doings for good.

They'll never come back to advance or attack ;

But, God ! don't we wish that they could !

RED WINE

Now seven supple lads and clean
   Sat down to drink one night,
Sat down to drink at Nouex-les-Mines
   And then went off to fight ;
And seven supple lads and clean
   Are finished with the fight,
But only three at Nouex-les-Mines
   Sit down to drink to-night.

And when we took the cobbled road
   We often took before,
Our thoughts were with the hearty lads
   Who trod that way no more.

Oh ! lads out on the level fields,

    If you could call to mind

The good red wine at Nouex-les-Mines

    You would not stay behind !

And when we left the trench to-night,

    Each weary with his load,

Grey, silent ghosts, as light as air,

    Came with us down the road.

And now we sit us down to drink

    You sit beside us, too,

And drink red wine at Nouex-les-Mines

    As once you used to do.

THE DAWN

(Givenchy.)

THE dawn comes creeping o'er the plains,
The saffron clouds are streaked with red,
I hear the creaking limber chains,
I see the drivers raise the reins
And urge their weary mules ahead.

And men go up and men go down,
The marching hosts are grand to see
In shrapnel-shivered trench and town,
In spinneys where the leaves of brown
Are falling on the dewy lea.

Lonely and still the village lies,
The houses sleeping, the blinds all drawn.

The road is straight as the bullet flies,

The villagers fix their waking eyes

On the shrapnel smoke that shrouds the

dawn.

Out of the battle, out of the night,

Into the dawn and the blush of day,

The road that takes us back from the fight,

The road we love, it is straight and white,

And it runs from the battle, away, away.

THE FLY

Buzz-fly and gad-fly, dragon-fly and blue,
When you're in the trenches come and visit
you,
They revel in your butter-dish and riot on your
ham,
Drill upon the army cheese and loot the
army jam.
They're with you in the dusk and the dawning
and the noon,
They come in close formation, in column and
platoon.
There's never zest like Tommy's zest when
these have got to die :
For Tommy takes his puttees off and strafs the
blooming fly.

OUT YONDER

You may see his eye shine brightly, for he bears
    his burden lightly,
As he makes his journey nightly up the long
    road from Bethune,
With his bayonet briskly swinging, and you'll
    hear him singing, singing,
In the silence and the silver, molten silver, of
    the moon.

Young and eager—bright his face is, spirit of
    the shrapneled places
Where the homes are battered, broken, and the
    land in ruin lies.

But the young adventure burning gives him
    never time for yearning,
And the natal flame of roving gleams like
    lightning in his eyes.

What awaits you, boy, out yonder, where the
    great guns rip and thunder ?
There's a menace in their message—guns that
    called you from afar.
But where'er your fortunes guide you may no
    woe or ill betide you—
Heaven speed you, little soldier, gaily going to
    the war.

I WILL GO BACK

I'LL go back again to my father's house and live
    on my father's land—
For my father's house is by Rosses' shore that
    slopes to Dooran strand,
And the wild mountains of Donegal rise up on
    either hand.

I have been gone from Donegal for seven years
    and a day,
And true enough it's a long, long while for a
    wanderer to stay—
But the hills of home are aye in my heart and
    never are far away.

The long white road winds o'er the hill from
Fanad to Kilcar,
And winds apast Gweebara Bay where the
deep sea-waters are—
Where the long grey boats go out by night to
fish beyond the bar.

I'll lie by the beach the livelong day, where the
foreshore dips to the sea—
When the sun is red on the golden gorse as once
it used to be ;
And, O ! but it's many an olden thought will
come up in the heart of me.

For the friends of my youth shall gather
around, the friends that I knew of old,
The olden songs will be sung to me and the old,
old stories told

Beside the fire of my father's house when the
    nights are long and cold.

'Tis there that I'll pass my years away, back in
    my native land ;
In my father's house by Rosses' shore that lies
    by Dooran strand,
Where the hills of ancient Donegal rise up on
    either hand.

THE FARMER'S BOY

[Every May, a great number of Donegal youths, whose ages range from twelve to fifteen years, go to the hiring fair of Strabane in the Co. Tyrone, and there, in the market-place, they are sold like cattle to the highest bidder. Their wages range from £3 to £5 for six months, and they have to work about eighteen hours a day.]

WHEN I went o'er the mountains a farmer's boy
to be,

My mother wept all morning when taking leave
of me ;

My heart was heavy in me, but I thrept that I
was gay :

A man of twelve should never weep when going
far away.

In the country o'er the mountains the rough
    roads straggle down,
There's many a long and weary mile 'twixt
    there and Glenties town ;
I went to be a farmer's boy, to work the season
    through,
From Whitsuntide to Hallowe'en, which time
    the rent came due

When virgin pure, the dawn's white arm stole
    o'er my mother's door,
From Glenties town I took the road I never
    trod before ;
Come Lammas tide I would not see the trout
    in Greenan's Burn,
And Hallowe'en might come and go, but I
    would not return.

My mother's love for me is warm ; her house
    is cold and bare :
A man who wants to see the world has little
    comfort there ;
And there 'tis hard to pay the rent, for all you
    dig and delve,
But there's hope beyond the mountains for a
    little man of twelve.

When I went o'er the mountains I worked for
    days on end,
Without a soul to cheer me through or one to
    call me friend ;
With older mates I toiled and toiled, in rain
    and heat and wind,
And kept my place. A Glenties man is never
    left behind.

The farmer's wench looked down on me, for she
　　　was spruce and clean,
But men of twelve don't care for girls like lads
　　　of seventeen ;
And sorrow take the farmer's wench ! her
　　　pride could never hold
With mine when hoeing turnip fields with
　　　fellows twice as old.

And so from May to Hallowe'en I wrought and
　　　felt content,
And sent my wages through the post to pay my
　　　mother's rent ;
For I kept up the Glenties name, and blest,
　　　when all was done,
The pride that gave a man of twelve the
　　　strength of twenty-one.

THE DUG-OUT

DEEPER than the daisies in the rubble and the
loam,

Wayward as a river the winding trenches
roam,

Past bowed, decrepit dug-outs leaning on their
props,

Beyond the shattered village where the
lightest limber stops ;

Through fields untilled and barren, and ripped
by shot and shell,—

The bloodstained braes of Souchez, the
meadows of Vermelles,

And poppies crown the parapet that rises from
   the mud—
   Where the soldiers' homes—the dug-outs—
   are built of clay and blood.

Our comrades on the level roofs, the dead men,
   waste away
   Upon the soldiers' frontier homes, the
   crannies in the clay ;
For on the meadows of Vermelles, and all the
   country round,
   The stiff and still stare at the skies, the quick
   are underground.

STRAF' THAT FLY

(Bully-Grenay.)

THERE's the butter, gad, and horse-fly,
The blow-fly and the blue,
The fine fly and the coarse fly,
But never flew a worse fly
Of all the flies that flew

Than the little sneaky black fly
That gobbles up our ham,
The beggar's not a slack fly,
He really is a crack fly,
And wolfs the soldiers' jam.

So straf' that fly ! our motto
Is " Straf' him when you can."
He'll die because he ought to,
He'll go because he's got to,
So at him, every man !

THE STAR-SHELL

(Loos.)

A star-shell holds the sky beyond
Shell-shivered Loos, and drops
In million sparkles on a pond
That lies by Hulluch copse.

A moment's brightness in the sky,
To vanish at a breath,
And die away, as soldiers die
Upon the wastes of death.

AFTER THE WAR

WHEN I come back to England,
   And times of Peace come round,
I'll surely have a shilling,
   And maybe have a pound.
I'll walk the whole town over,
   And who shall say me nay,
For I'm a British soldier
   With a British soldier's pay.

I only joined for fun,
   Never joined for profit—
The Army pay is good,
   But, God! there's little of it.

When I come back to England

    I won't be half a swell—

Ribbons for the scrapping

    At Loos and New Chapelle.

I'll search the whole town over

    To find another trade,

And be a blooming boot-black

    On Charing Cross parade.

I will not leave for fun—

    The change will bring me profit.

The Army pay is good,

    But, God! there's little of it.

A SOLDIER'S PRAYER

GIVENCHY village lies a wreck, Givenchy
    Church is bare,

No more the peasant maidens come to say
    their vespers there.

The altar rails are wrenched apart, with rubble
    littered o'er,

The sacred, broken sanctuary-lamp lies smashed
    upon the floor ;

And mute upon the crucifix He looks upon it
    all—

The great white Christ, the shrapnel-scourged,
    upon the eastern wall.

He sees the churchyard delved by shells, the
tombstones flung about,

And dead men's skulls, and white, white bones
the shells have shovelled out ;

The trenches running line by line through
meadow fields of green,

The bayonets on the parapets, the wasting
flesh between ;

Around Givenchy's ruined church the levels,
poppy-red,

Are set apart for silent hosts, the legions of
the dead.

And when at night on sentry-go, with danger
keeping tryst,

I see upon the crucifix the blood-stained form
of Christ

Defiled and maimed, the merciful on vigil all
the time,

Pitying his children's wrath, their passion and
their crime.

Mute, mute He hangs upon His Cross, the
symbol of His pain,

And as men scourged Him long ago, they
scourge Him once again—

There in the lonely war-lit night to Christ the
Lord I call,

"Forgive the ones who work Thee harm. O
Lord, forgive us all."

DUG-OUT PROVERBS

HERE are the Old Sweats sayings. He tells the
   tale of his trade—
Gleanings from trench and dug-out, battle,
   fatigue, parade.

'Tis said the Boche has pluck enough. Of this
   I have no doubt,
But see him in the darkest light until you've
   knocked him out.

Your dug-out took you hours to build. Got
   broken in a minute !
A rotten shame ! Be thankful, son, your carcass
   isn't in it.

And if one shelters you a night tend it roof and
    rafter,
And make it better than it was—for those who
    follow after.

" The trench is calm," you say, my son. The
    Boche is keeping quiet.
Then keep your rifle close at hand. We soon
    shall have a riot.

A soldier's life is risky ; it may end damn quick.
    Well, let it !
Since we get five francs every week we'll burst
    it when we get it.

You may cough and sneeze in your dug-out,
    but you can't go anywhere.
There's little health around the house—the dead
    are lying there.

You may dig as deep as a spade can dig, but
    the Boche's eye can tell
Where the khaki moles have plied their trade,
    and the beggars burrow well.

Pray to God when the dirt* flies over and the
    country flops about,
But stick to your dug-out all the same until
    you're ordered out.

When guns are going large a bit and sending
    gifts from Krupp,
You've got to keep your napper low, but keep
    your spirits up.

These are the dug-out maxims which the " Old
    Sweats " fling about,
For the better education of the " rooky " newly
    out.

* Dirt.   Trench term for shells.